THE PHILOKALIA

ΦΙΛΟΚΑΛΙΑ

ΤΩΝ ΙΕΡΩΝ

ΝΗΠΤΙΚΩΝ·

ΣΥΝΕΡΑΝΙΣΘΕΙΣΑ

ΠΑΡΑ ΤΩΝ ΑΓΙΩΝ ΚΑΙ ΘΕΟΦΟΡΩΝ

ΠΑΤΕΡΩΝ ΗΜΩΝ

ΕΝ Η͂,

Διὰ τῆς κỳ τὴ Πρᾶξιν κỳ Θεωρίαν Ἠθικῆς Φιλο-
σοφίας ὁ νῦς καθαίρεται, φωτίζεται, κỳ τελειῦται

ΕΠΙΜΕΛΕΙᾼ ΜΕ᾽Ν ΟΤΙ ΠΛΕΙΣΤῌ ΔΙΟΡΘΩΘΕΙΣᾺ·

ΝΤ͂Ν ΔΕ᾽ ΠΡΩΤΟΝ ΤΥΠΟΙΣ ΕΚΔΟΘΕΙΣΑ

ΔΙΑ ΔΑΠΑΝΗΣ

ΤΟΥ ΤΙΜΙΩΤΑΤΟΥ, ΚΑΙ ΘΕΟΣΕΒΕΣΤΑΤΟΥ ΚΥΡΙΟΥ

ΙΩΑΝΝΟΥ ΜΑΥΡΟΓΟΡΔΑΤΟΥ

ΕΙΣ ΚΟΙΝΗΝ ΤΩΝ ΟΡΘΟΔΟΞΩΝ ΩΦΕΛΕΙΑΝ.

αψπβ. ΕΝΕΤΙΗΣΙΝ, 1782.

ΠΑΡΑ ΑΝΤΩΝΙΩ, ΤΩ ΒΟΡΤΟΛΙ,

CON LICENZA DE' SUPERIORI, E PRIVILEGIO.

THE PHILOKALIA

Writings of Holy Mystic Fathers in which
is Explained how the Mind is Purified,
Illumined, and Perfected through Practical
and Contemplative Ethical Philosophy

Compiled by
ST. MACARIOS OF CORINTH
and edited by
ST. NICODEMOS THE HAGIORITE

Translated from the
original Greek and Edited by
CONSTANTINE CAVARNOS

INSTITUTE FOR BYZANTINE
AND MODERN GREEK STUDIES
115 Gilbert Road
Belmont, Massachusetts 02478-2200
U.S.A.

First Edition, 2008
All Rights Reserved
Copyright, © 2007 by Constantine Cavarnos
Published by THE INSTITUTE FOR BYZANTINE
AND MODERN GREEK STUDIES, INC.
115 Gilbert Road
Belmont, Massachusetts 02478-2200

Library of Congress Control Number: 2007940036

Printed in the United States of America

Clothbound ISBN 1-884729-79-7

CONTENTS

INTRODUCTION
By CONSTANTINE CAVARNOS

Two books are known by the title of *Philokalia* (Φιλοκαλία), a Greek term which means "love for what is beautiful." One of them is a compilation from the writings of Origen (c. 185-254) made in the fourth century by St. Basil the Great and St. Gregory Nazianzen. The other is an anthology of writings by some thirty Mystic Fathers, ranging from the fourth to the fifteenth century, compiled and edited by two holy men of the Eastern Orthodox Church: St. Macarios Notaras (1731-1805), Archbishop of Corinth, and St. Nicodemos the Hagiorite (1749-1809). The full title of the second *Philokalia*, with which we are concerned here, is *Philokalia of Our Holy Mystic Fathers*. It has the subtitle: "In Which It Is Explained How the Mind is Purified, Illumined, and Perfected through Practical and Contemplative Ethical Philosophy."

The term "love for what is beautiful" signifies in this work love of *spiritual beauty*: the love of the beauty of God, the love of the beauty of the soul, of its virtues, and the love of the most beautiful way of life, the spiritual.

Saints Macarios and Nicodemos viewed the *Philokalia* which they compiled, edited, and published, as a philosophical work, because it teaches practices that were called philosophical during the Byzantine period, when the texts gathered in the *Philokalia* were written. These practices are inner attention, guarding of the senses and of the imagination, and mental prayer. They were called "philosophy," "internal philosophy" and "spiritual philosophy," and were contrasted to "external" or "secular" philosophy."[1]

Macarios compiled the first text of the *Philokalia*, and when he visited the Holy Mountain of Athos in 1777, he gave it to the monk Nicodemos to complete and edit. Nicodemos added, among other things, an Introduction and Brief Biographies of the Fathers whose writings are included in this work. He had it ready for the printer after two years, during which he also edited other manuscripts that Macarios had submitted to him: one entitled *Evergetinos*, and another, *Concerning Continual Communion*. When all three were ready, Macarios took them and left for Smyrna, where he hoped he would find donors to

[1] See my book *The Hellenic-Christian Philosophical Tradition*, pp. 109-114.

pay for the printing. He was successful, and the three books were published in Venice. *The Philokalia* appeared in 1782; the other two, in the following year. John Mavrogordatos, prince of Moldo-Wallachia, financed the printing of the *Philokalia*. His name appears on the title page and in the Proem of this monumental work of 1,207 folio pages.

The *Philokalia* was destined to exert a profound influence on the spiritual life, first of Greece, and soon of the entire Orthodox world. It was reprinted at Constantinople in 1861, and at Athens in 1893, 1900, and during the period 1957-1963. The latter edition is in five volumes. The impact of the *Philokalia* on the Slavonic world was so strong that eleven years after its first publication a Slavonic version came out in Moscow, under the title of *Dobrotolubiye*. The translator was the Russian monk Paissy Velichkovsky, who had gone to Mount Athos in 1746, stayed there for seventeen years, and then settled in Moldavia, a part of present-day Rumania. He and his disciples are credited with the spiritual revival that took place in Russia at the end of the eighteenth century and the beginning of the nineteenth. Between 1876 and 1890, a five-volume Russian version of the *Philokalia* was published. The translation was made by the

Russian bishop Theophan the Recluse, with the help of some monks of the Monastery of Optino and the Theological Academy of Moscow.

The strong influence of the *Philokalia* upon the Russians is also manifest in *Candid Narratives of a Pilgrim to His Spiritual Father* (Kazan, 1884). This work, appeared in English under the title of *The Way of a Pilgrim*. This is one of the finest and most popular manuals of Eastern Orthodox spirituality. It was written in the second half of the nineteenth century by an unknown author inspired by the *Philokalia*.

In recent years, the *Philokalia* has appeared in Rumanian, German, English, and French. An English version, in two volumes, was translated by E. Kadloubovsky and G. E. H. Palmer from the Russian. The first volume, entitled *Writings from the Philokalia on Prayer of the Heart*, was published in 1951, while the second volume, *Early Fathers from the Philokalia*, came out in 1954. Another English language version, in four volumes, made from the latest Greek edition mentioned above, appeared in London between 1981 and 1995.

The Greek *Philokalia* contains the works of about thirty writers, most of them saints of the Eastern Church, some well known, others less, some anonymous. The sequence in which they are presented is on the whole chronological. The Slavonic *Dobrotolubiye* is an abridged version of the *Philokalia*, containing fewer than half of the authors. They are arranged according to type rather than in strictly chronological sequence.

The Russian *Dobrotolubiye* is appreciably larger than the Greek *Philokalia*. Although it entirely omits four of the authors in the Greek *Philokalia*, some chapters by Palamas, and two of the anonymous texts, it adds nine other writers. The order in which they appear is different again from that of the Greek *Philokalia*.

The early two-volume English version of the *Philokalia*, consists of selections from volumes I, II, III, and V of the Russian *Dobrotolubiye*. The new English edition, made from the 1957-1963 Greek edition, has not been completed. The Rumanian edition (1946-1948, 1976-1981), by Professor Dumitru Staniloae, is an expanded one of ten volumes. It includes many writings which are not in the Greek edition. For instance, texts by St. Isaac the Syrian, St. John Climacos, and Abba Dorotheos.

In the discussion of the *Philokalia* that follows, I shall rely on the Athens edition of 1957-1963. This includes all the texts contained in the first edition, arranged in the same order, plus some extra chapters by Patriarch Kallistos. It is divided into five volumes. My aim is to indicate and briefly explain the main teachings contained in it.

To help man attain his own highest spiritual perfection is the ultimate goal of the *Philokalia*. The methods, both physical and spiritual, for attaining this end, are its principal matter. The path to be followed is spoken of as "the science *(epistéme)* of sciences and the art *(téchne)* of arts."

To understand this art or science one must have some acquaintance with the concept of human nature which it presupposes. Man is seen as God's supreme creature: everything was created for him. "Man alone of all creatures on earth," says St. John Damascene, "is in the image and likeness of God." The terms "in the image" *(kat' eikóna)* and "in the likeness" *(kath' homoíosin)* are given a distinct meaning in the *Philokalia*. "Every man," says this saint, "is in the *image* of God, because of his possession of reason *(nous)* and of a soul which is incomprehensible, invisible, immortal, free, fit for rule, creative.... But very few men are in the *likeness* of God: only the virtuous and saints, who imitate God's goodness so far as is possible for man."

Man is a dual being, composed of body *(sóma)* and soul *(psyché)*. The soul is an incorporeal, rational, immortal substance *(ousía)*, superior to the body. "It does not occupy a place," says St. Gregory Palamas, "but neither is it everywhere.... It is throughout the body, not as being in a place, nor as being contained, but as holding the body together, containing it, and giving life to it." The soul sustains all the members of the body, gives life to them, and moves them. When it departs from the body, the body dies.

The soul has diverse faculties or powers *(dynámeis)*, including reason, will, conscience, and imagination. *Reason*, usually referred to as *nous* or *logistikón*, has two distinct aspects, the contemplative or intuitive, generally called *nous,* and the discursive, most often denoted by the term *diánoia.* Palamas distinguishes between the "essence" *(ousía)* of the rational faculty and its "energy" or operation *(enérgeia).* The energy consists of mental events, such as thoughts, while the essence is the power that produces these. Reason is the highest faculty in man. It is the governor *(kybernétes)* or master *(autokrátor)* of the whole man, free in its activity. It is the faculty not only of knowledge, but also of inner attention or observation *(prosoché)* and of contemplation *(theoría).* It can observe itself as well as what is distinct from itself. Its power of attention renders it the guardian of the whole man. Through attention, *nous* observes evil and undesirable thoughts, images, desires, and feelings, and opposes them. The highest activity of the rational faculty is pure prayer.

In its truly natural state, reason can intuitively apprehend higher truth and behold the uncreated Divine light. It is in its natural state when it is pure, free of bad or useless thoughts and feelings. Such reason is very rare; it is possessed only by saints. Hence, strictly speaking, they alone are truly rational. "For one to be or become rational *(logikós)* in accordance with nature, as man originally was," says St. Gregory the Sinaite, "is impossible before the attainment of purity and incorruptibility.... They alone are actually rational who through purity have become saints."

The will *(thélesis, boúlesis)* is an active power characterized by the freedom of choice, the freedom to incline either towards the good or towards evil. A free act of the will, whereby it surrenders itself to the Divine will, is the beginning of the process of salvation *(soteria)*. St. Peter Damascene remarks: "Free choice is the beginning of salvation. This choice consists in man's giving up his own volitions and thoughts, and doing the thoughts and volitions of God." "The ascent and deification of the will," says St. Theodore of Edessa, "consists in its complete and continuous inclination and movement towards the

Supremely Beautiful. The turning of the will towards God comes as a free act of the human will, not as a result of Divine constraint. In his fallen state, man needs Grace to *strengthen* the will's inclination and movement upwards. However, the initial act of turning from the lower to the higher must come from man, his freedom being inviolable.

Conscience (*syneídesis*) occupies a very important place in the *Philokalia*. This faculty is a true teacher that counsels excellently as to what is conducive to our salvation. It tells us what we ought to do, what our duties and obligations are. According to St. Mark the Ascetic, "Conscience is a natural book and he who reads it and follows it in practice gains the experience of divine perception." Conscience resists acts that are contrary to nature, and censures us when we perform them. In man's ordinary state, conscience is more or less inoperative, having been separated from consciousness. It needs to be awakened and united with the rest of man's faculties. Conscience is awakened by Divine grace; but grace operates in proportion as we live in accordance with the Commandments. Also, except in the case of the saint, conscience is impure. Its purification is effected especially through inner wakefulness or attention combined with prayer.

The imagination *(phantasía) is* one of the lower psy-
chical faculties of man. It operates in a realm between
reason and sense, and is also possessed by irrational
animals. Imagination is divided into proper and improper. The first is accessory to meditation, as when
one conjures up a picture of the Final Judgment in order to escape from base and evil thoughts. Improper
imagination is that which is occupied with worldly,
demonic, and unbecoming things. Imagination is
one of the main obstacles to pure prayer, which requires an undistracted mind. It is also the chief instrument evil spirits use in leading man to wrong
thinking, wrong feeling, and wrong doing. This is
effected through suggestion *(prosbolé)*. If suggestion
is not consciously observed by means of inner attention and it is not opposed by the mind, it results in
an identification *(syndyasmós)* with it, next in consent
(synkatáthesis), and finally in the sinful act *(práxis tes
hamartías)*. In striving to practice pure prayer of the
heart, say the Fathers of the *Philokalia,* one should
suppress the imagination entirely, not only improper, but proper imagination as well. That is, the mind
must be kept free of all images, both good and bad.

What is said in the *Philokalia* about reason, the will,
conscience, the imagination, and the senses, shows
that man in his ordinary, so-called normal state, is

far from being what he ought to be. He is separated from higher truth and the Divine by various forms of impurity, and is kept chained to lower levels of experience and being. Man is in need of what the "Wakeful Fathers" (*Neptikoí Patéres*) call the "beautiful" or "good" change *(alloíosis)*, which is growth in likeness to God leading to union with Him, to deification *(théosis)*. This change is to be brought about by means of "work" *(ergasía)* or "training" *(áskesis)*. "Bodily work" consists of such practices as fasting, continence, vigils, prostrations, and standing motionless at prayer. "Spiritual work" consists of concentration, meditation, inner attention, mental prayer and other interior practices. The expression "Practical and Contemplative Ethical Philosophy," which appears in the subtitle of the *Philokalia*, refers to such bodily and spiritual work.

In order to bring about the desired transformation, "work" must be performed with great diligence and energy. Hence the bodily and spiritual practices are often referred to as "voluntary suffering" *(hekoúsioi pónoi)*. The necessity of performing these activities in such a manner is very clearly indicated in the following passage by St. Gregory the Sinaite: "No work, whether bodily or spiritual, which lacks pain or effort, ever produces fruit. For 'the kingdom of heaven suffers violence,' says the Lord, 'and the violent take it by force.'"

The *Philokalia*, however, is chiefly concerned with *spiritual* practices, and it is with these and their results that we shall deal in the remainder of this Introduction. Of the bodily practices, it will only be noted that the writers in the *Philokalia* regard them as important *instruments* for the spiritual practices, but not of value in themselves.

Concentration *(synagogé)* as a mental practice is of fundamental importance. It is an essential component in the arts of meditation, inner attention, and mental prayer. The rational faculty has the tendency to wander about *(meteorízesthai)* in "the world," to be distracted by sense-objects, images, and thoughts. Christ, we are reminded, urges us to avoid this wandering. "Our Lord," observes St. Symeon the New Theologian, "tells us in the Holy Gospel: `Avoid being distracted *(me meteorízesthai)*,' that is, do not scatter your mind hither and thither. And in another place He says: `Blessed are the poor in spirit;' that is, fortunate are those who have not acquired in their heart any worldly cares, but are destitute of every worldly thought." Concentration is the withdrawing of the mind from the external world, turning it inward, gathering it into the heart. The effect of concentration is an intensification of the mind's contemplative power. With regard to this point, Kallistos, Patriarch of Constantinople (fl. 1360), observes: "In proportion as the mind draws itself together, it becomes receptive of greater things. And when, drawing together all its movements, whether discursive, intuitive, or any other whatsoever, restraining them, then it beholds Him Who is great beyond all else: God. And it beholds Him in proportion as the all-holy Grace of the Spirit grants, and as the nature of that which inhabits matter and is created can see Him Who is outside these."

Withdrawing from worldly objects into the heart, the mind should meditate, exercise inner attention, and pray. Meditation *(meléte)* is the focusing of the mind on God, death, judgment, hell, heaven, the lives of saints, the words of Christ, the apothegms of the Fathers, and the like. Regarding meditation on God, St. Peter Damascene says: "One ought to meditate on the name of God more often than one breathes, at every time and place, and whatever one is doing." And St. Symeon the New Theologian advises: "Have the mind always turned to God, both in sleep and while awake, both when you are eating and when you are talking, both when you are doing manual work or are engaged in any other activity." Such meditation

causes one to rejoice within, forgetting worldly afflictions and becoming free from cares.

Meditation on death is connected with meditation on the judgment, on heaven and hell. "He who
has acquired memory of death as a companion," remarks the same Father, "will seek with painful efforts to learn what awaits him after his departure
from this life." This meditation results in non-attach-
ment *(aprospátheia)* to present things, indispensable
for perfect knowledge of future things.

Insofar as it consists in remembering God, meditation is an essential element of prayer. Otherwise
it is a *preparation* of the mind for prayer. "When the
mind has become languid from [long continued]
prayer," says Theoleptos (fl. 1325), "renew its power
by means of reading and meditation, and make it
readier for prayer."

The highest form of spiritual work is mental
prayer *(noerá proseuché)*, prayer of the heart *(kardiaké
proseuché)*, or pure prayer *(kathará proseuché)*. This
form of prayer is called "mental prayer" because it is
carried on entirely by the mind or spiritual faculty;
"prayer of the heart," because the mind engages in it
while concentrated in the heart; and "pure prayer,"
because it presupposes a mind and heart free of fantasies and thoughts. During this prayer, one invokes

Jesus Christ, saying: "Lord Jesus Christ, Son of God, have mercy upon me." Hence it is also known as "the Jesus Prayer" *(euché Iesoú, epíklesis Iesoú).*

Mental prayer should be practiced as far as possible incessantly, not only by monks, to whom the *Philokalia* is especially addressed, but by all Christians, in accordance with the precept of the Apostle Paul (in the *First Epistle to the Thessalonians*) to "pray without ceasing." Although it can be practiced at any place and in any posture, it is most easily and successfully practiced—particularly by beginners—when one is seated in a dark, quiet place, with the head lowered. The reason why such a place and position are best is that they aid concentration, an essential for successful prayer.

At each drawing of the breath one utters mentally the words: "Lord Jesus Christ, Son of God, have mercy upon me." To be really fruitful, this prayer must be practiced in the right manner over a long period. One cannot practice it correctly unless he carefully follows the instructions in authoritative books and has the guidance of a wise and experienced spiritual guide.

The first notable result of this prayer is pleasant warmth *(thérme)* of the heart, which purifies man of passions, effecting a state of passionlessness. This warmth is a manifestation of God, of Divine love. It "is the fire which our Lord Jesus Christ came to cast upon the earth of our hearts," remark Kallistos and Ignatios Xanthopouloi. The "passions" constitute a dividing wall *(mesóteichon)* between the heart and God, which darkens it and separates the mind from God. The overcoming and uprooting of the passions, the removal of the dividing wall or barrier, in a word passionlessness *(apátheia)*, opens the heart and mind to God. Through the opening of the heart *(kardiakón ánoigma)* the Divine light enters us. First, then, comes warmth of the heart, then illumination *(photismós)* or effulgence *(éllampsis)*. Illumination is "an ineffable energy, which is seen invisibly and known unknowably," according to Kallistos and Ignatios Xanthopouloi. Palamas, who deals most extensively with illumination, says: "The Divine and deifying effulgence and grace is not the essence of God, but His uncreated energy *(áktistos enérgeia)*." This light is also identified by him and other Fathers with the beauty *(kállos)* of God. The title of the *Philokalia*, which, as we have noted, means "love for what is beautiful," is due in part to this identification. Our love *(philía, agápe, eros)* should be directed above all to God, Whose most entrancing aspect is that of ineffable beauty. Kallistos and Ignatios quote St. Basil the Great on this point: "What is more wonderful than the Divine beauty? What conception of God's magnificence is more glorious? What aspiration of the soul is so ardent and unbearable as that which is engendered by God in a soul ·which has been purified of every vice and which from a true disposition says: `I am wounded by love?'." The *Philokalia* is termed "love for what is beautiful" also because it is directed to the virtues, which the writers in it view as beautiful qualities that reflect the beauty of God.

Through prayer of the heart a union *(hénosis)* is achieved of man with himself and with God. Warmth of the heart, by consuming the passions, which are dividing forces, brings about the integration of the powers of the soul. Also, this warmth, being Divine love or grace appropriated in us, unites the soul with God. Similarly illumination, as a vision of, and union with, the Divine light, is a union with God, Who is light.

Union with God, or *théosis,* admits of degrees. It depends on the degree of the capacity of receiving it, that is, on purity of soul and likeness to God. Perfection with respect to such union is of two levels, the relative and the absolute. The latter is not attainable in this life.

These fruits of interior prayer are impossible with-

out inner wakefulness *(népsis)* or attention *(prosoché)*.
Evagrios of Pontos (died 399) remarks : "Prayer which
is not practiced inwardly, in a wakeful, vigilant state,
is really futile." To be effective, prayer must be pure;
and it is pure when the imagination is suppressed,
and the mind and heart are free of thoughts, images, and passions. As inner attention brings about
these results, it is characterized by St. Nikephoros
the Solitary (fl. 1340) as "the beginning of contemplation, or rather the foundation of contemplation."
Inner wakefulness is a higher level of consciousness
(aísthesis), transcending ordinary consciousness,
which is really a state of inner sleep *(hypnos)*, of inner unawareness *(anaisthesía)*. Our ordinary waking
consciousness is a passive state of inner sleep, in that
it is characterized by lack of a detached awareness of
the contents or events of our mind, heart, and imagination, and the promptings of conscience. Inner
wakefulness is an active state of mind, characterized
by an objective awareness of these, that is, by self-ob-
servation, self-awareness. Because the writers in the
Philokalia stress this fact and dwell upon the practice of inner wakefulness or *népsis*, they are called
"Wakeful Fathers," *Neptikoí Patéres.*

The sources of this teaching and the emphasis
given to it in the *Philokalia* are to be found in the

New Testament. They appear in statements made by Christ and by the Apostle Paul. One very important and illuminating passage appears in *Matthew* 26:41, a statement made by Christ in Gethsemane before the Betrayal. Christ said to His disciples: "Be wakeful (*gregoreíte*) and pray (*proseúchesthe*) that you enter not into temptation." Very important here is the fact that Christ links "being wakeful" with "praying." The Fathers of the *Philokalia* do the same. Significant also is the fact that again and again our Lord uses the verb *gregoreíte,* urging His listeners to be wakeful in various situations. St. Paul, too, in his *Epistles,* urges his readers to be wakeful in all other things too. Thus, in his *Epistle to the Colossians* he says: "Continue in prayer, being wakeful in it (*te proseuché gregoroúntes*)."[1] Paul also employs the verb *népho* (νήφω), which is a synonym of *gregoréo.* He also uses the adjectval form of this term: *nephálios* (νηφάλιος),[2] which appears in the *Philokalia* in important contexts.

Although wakefulness is particularly emphasized as important in praying, it is viewed as relevant in *all* our activities. Thus, in the *Second Epistle to Timothy*

[1] 4:2.
[2] *1 Timothy* 3:2, 11.
[3] *2 Timothy* 4:5.

he says: "Be wakeful in all things."[3] Having the same root as the verb *népho* is the noun *népsis* (νῆψις), which is much used in the *Philokalia,* but does not appear in the *New Testament.* It is employed in the *Philokalia* to denote *inner attention* or *wakefulness* directed particularly to thoughts, fantasies, and passions, and as synonymous with *prosoché* "attention." In the *New Testament* the activity of the mind called *prosoché* appears many times in the verb form, *prosécho.* It is emphasized in the *Philokalia* that in order to be successful, prayer must be conjoined with inner attention—without it prayer is fruitless.

Concerning the manner in which inner wakefulness or attention should be joined to prayer of the heart, St. Symeon the New Theologian says: "Attention must be so united to prayer as the body is to the soul.... Attention must go forward and observe the enemies like a scout, and it must first engage in combat with sin, and resist the bad thoughts that come to the soul. Prayer must follow attention, banishing and destroying at once all the evil thoughts which attention previously fought, because by itself attention cannot destroy them."[1] Thus practiced, this prayer, which is called "mental prayer" and "prayer of the heart," leads to a higher level of consciousness, in some measure to theosis.

[1] Φιλοκαλία, Vol. 5, Athens, 1963, p. 81.

PROEM

By ST. NICODEMOS THE HAGIORITE

God, the Blessed Nature, the Transcendent Perfection, the Creative Principle of all good and beautiful things, Transcendently Good and Beautiful, having from eternity destined according to His Divine Idea to deify man, and having from the beginning within Himself set this purpose, created man at a time when He was well pleased.

Making the body out of matter and placing inside it a soul which He created, He set man as a sort of a cosmos, great by virtue of the soul's many and superior powers, in a small cosmos. He placed man as a contemplator of Visible Creation and as an initiate of Intelligible Creation, according to the Gregory who is great in Theology.[1] And what else but as really a statue and a divinely made image full of all the graces. And having given him the Law of the Commandments as a kind of test of his power of free

---

[1] St. Gregory, bishop of Nazianzus (c. 329-390).

27

choice and self-control. And as Sirach says, He left man in the power of his own deliberation,[1] to choose according to his own opinion in each situation. And as a prize, to receive the hypostatic gift of theosis, becoming God[2] and shining eternally with the purest Light.

But alas! The envy of the cunning wickedness of the introducer of evil from the beginning did not bear to see this take place. He was filled with envy against the Creator and His creature, as holy Maximos[3] says. Against the Creator, in order that His all-praiseworthy Goodness which created man might not be made manifest; against man, in order that man might not become a partaker of the supernal glory of theosis. By means of cunning, the Cunning One outwitted wretched man and made him transgress the deifying Commandment of God by means of pretended good counsel. And having separated man from Divine glory, the rebel seemed to himself to be an Olympic victor, because he had succeeded in interrupting the fulfillment of the eternal Will of God.

However, according to Divine revelation, the Will of God for the divinization of human nature abides

---

[1] *Wisdom of Sirach* 15:14 (Septuagint).
[2] In the sense of participating in God's "energies."
[3] Maximos the Confessor (d. 662).

forever. And thoughts in the heart of man regarding this continue generation after generation.[1] That is, statements regarding Providence and the Judgment which tend towards this aim, continued unchanged century after century, as the discussions of holy Maximos show. Consistently with this, in recent times, through deep compassion, the Divine Logos of the Father deigned to set aside the wishes of the Rulers of Darkness, and to actualize His ancient and true plan. Therefore, with the good pleasure of the Father and the synergy of the Holy Spirit, He became incarnate. He took on all of our nature and divinized it. And having offered His salvific and deifying Commandments, and through Baptism having sowed in our hearts the perfect Grace of the Holy Spirit like a divine seed, He gave to us, according to the divine Evangelist, authority, by living according to His life-giving Commandments and preserving unextinguished within us Divine grace, finally to bear fruits, becoming through it children of God and divinized, "coming unto a perfect man, unto the measure of the stature of the fullness of Christ."[2] This, briefly, is the whole end and conclusion of the Divine Dispensation.

[1] *Psalms* 32:11.
[2] *Ephesians* 4:13.

Alas, however! For it is proper at this point to sigh bitterly, according to divine Chrysostom.[1] For, as a result of ignorance and mostly blinded by worldly cares, we covered up Grace by the passions, so that it is in danger of being completely vanishing. We are almost the same as those who replied to the Apostle Paul that they never even heard that there is a Holy Spirit.[2] And there has truly happened to us what had happened earlier, according to the Prophet,[3] when men were not ruled by Grace.

Alas, our sickness! Would that our wickedness and our excessive attachment to visible things disappear! What is to be wondered at is that if we hear that Grace is active in others, we begrudge those who say this, and we believe that there is no active Grace in the present age. What then? The Spirit bestows wisdom upon the Godly wise Fathers and reveals to them general inner watchfulness and attention with regard to all things, and guarding of the mind. And He reveals to them the way to find Grace at once, a way that is wonderful and most scientific. This is the practice of praying unceasingly to our Lord Jesus Christ, the Son of God.[4] I mean not simply with the

[1] St. John Chrysostom (c. 347-407).
[2] *Acts of the Apostles* 19:2.
[3] *Isaiah* 63:16.
[4] *Luke* 17:21.

mind and the lips (this is obvious to all who choose to lead a pious life and is easy to anyone), but returning the whole mind to the inner man, and in the depths of the heart invoking the All-holy name of the Lord, asking for His mercy. One pays attention only to the bare words of the prayer and to nothing else whatsoever, whether external or internal, and keeps the mind altogether formless and colorless.

The occasion for this practice, its matter, so to speak, the holy Fathers took from the teaching of the Lord, Who said: "The Kingdom of God is within you;" and at other times He said: "Hypocrite, cleanse first that which is within the cup and platter, that the outside of them may be clean also."[1] This is to be understood not with regard to physical things but with regard to our inner man. From the Apostle Paul we may take the following, which appears in his *Epistle to the Ephesians*: "For this cause I bow my knees unto the Father of our Lord Jesus Christ.... That He would grant you to be strengthened with the might of His Spirit in the inner man; that Christ may dwell in your hearts by faith."[2] What could be clearer than this testimony? And elsewhere, he says: "Speaking to yourselves in psalms and hymns and

[1] *Matthew* 23:26.
[2] *Ephesians* 3:14-17.

spiritual songs, singing and making melody in your heart to the Lord."[1] Do you hear? "In your heart," he says. And the Apostle Peter adds this: "Until the day dawn, and the day star arise in your hearts."[2] That this is necessary for every pious person is taught by the Holy Spirit in countless other places of the New Testament, as can be ascertained by those who study them carefully.

By means of this spiritual and studious work, together with a life that is in accord with the Commandments and the moral virtues, through the warmth and energy that arise in the heart by means of the invocation of the All-holy name of Christ, the passions are consumed—"for our God is fire that consumeth" wickedness[3]—and the mind and the heart are gradually purified and are united with one another. When these are purified and united with one another, the salvific Commandments are more easily fulfilled. Thereby, the fruits of the Holy Spirit appear in the soul, and an abundance of blessings is lavished upon it.

To sum up, thereby it is possible to return faster to

[1] *Ephesians* 5:19.
[2] *2 Peter* 1:19.
[3] *Deuteronomy* 4:24.

the Grace that was bestowed at Baptism. This Grace was in us, but was like a spark in soot, covered up by the passions. Now it flashes resplendently, so that the soul is illumined and consequently perfected and deified.

This spiritual work is mentioned by most of the Fathers here and there in their writings. They speak about it as to persons who know about it. Some of them, perhaps foreseeing the ignorance and neglect of our generation regarding this salvific spiritual practice, explained in detail the manner in which it is to be practiced by means of certain natural methods. They exerted themselves to leave these methods as a fatherly heritage to us their descendents. They glorify it, employing many laudatory terms. They call this work "the beginning of every other God-pleasing practice," an "abundance of good things," "the purest distinguishing characteristic of repentance," and "a spiritual practice which constitutes an ascent to true contemplation." They exhort all to engage in this spiritually very profitable work.

I lament the present situation, and my emotion halts my speech. Almost all the books that philosophize about this "work," which Dionysios the Areopagite calls "illuminating and perfecting," have disappeared. It is mentioned in philosophizing books as well as in others that speak of *attention* and *inner wakefulness*. All speak of these as means and instruments that tend towards the same aim: to deify man. These books are very rare, owing to the passage of time and the fact that they have never appeared in print. If certain ones have survived somewhere, they are moth-eaten and corrupt, and almost the same as if they had never existed. I shall add that most of our fellow men are indifferent towards such works. And while they trouble themselves about many things—I mean the bodily and practical virtues, or, to speak more truly, they concern themselves with the *instruments* of the virtues—they spend their whole life occupied with these, and neglect the *one* thing that is most needed, that is, the *guarding of the mind and pure prayer*. I do not know whether they neglect the practice of guarding the mind and pure prayer because they do not know about them, or due to something else. This very sweet work is in danger of completely disappearing and as result, Grace is in danger of being obscured and extinguished, and, consequently our union with God, or theosis, is in danger of not taking place. (Which union, as we said earlier, was from the beginning the Will of God.) This union is the final goal towards which are directed the creation of the world and the Dispensation of the Logos of

God for our well-being, both temporal and eternal. And in general, it is the final goal of everything that has been done in a Divine manner in the Old and the New Testaments.

Formerly, many who lived in the "world," including Kings who dwelt in Kingdoms and daily had myriads of cares and concerns, had one essential work, to pray unceasingly in their heart. We find many such instances in history. At present, due to negligence and ignorance, not only among those in the world, but also among monastics, this is something very rare. Oh the loss! Deprived of this, although each one struggles as far as possible for the acquisition of virtue and endures the accompanying hardships, still one reaps no fruit. For without the unceasing remembrance of the Lord, and purity of the heart and mind from everything evil—a purity generated by this practice—it is impossible to bear fruit. Christ says: "Without Me ye can do nothing;" and again: "He that abideth in Me, bringeth forth much fruit."[1]

Wherefore, I surmise that there is no other explanation for the present absence of individuals who are distinguished for holiness during their lifetime and

[1] *John* 15.5.

after death, which means that few are saved in this age.[1] The reason for this is the neglect of this practice which elevates to theosis. Without the divinization of the mind, someone has said, it is impossible for one to become a saint or even to be saved. Only to hear that according to those who are divinely wise salvation and theosis are the same thing, is frightening. Moreover, what is most important, we lack books that teach us how to strive for theosis. Without these, to succeed in this endeavor is something impossible.

Behold, however, the ever truly good and noble and Christ-loving Kyrios Ioannis Mavrogordatos, surpassing all in liberality, in love for the poor, in hospitality, and in the rest of the choir of the virtues, always filled with divine zeal to benefit the public, inspired by the Grace of Christ Who wants all men to be saved and divinized, changed our lament to joy, freeing us from the impass. With his whole soul he puts before the public the means of theosis, and so to speak with both hands and feet he helps and contributes by every means to this end, to the pre-eternal—as has been said above—plan of God.

---

[1] Cf. *Luke* 13:23.

This is glory! This is magnificence! Behold the manuscripts lying here and there in obscure corners, moth-eaten and despised. Behold these texts which guide us systematically to purity of the heart, to watchfulness of the mind, to the recovery of Grace within us, and, theosis. Behold them all gathered together, being handed over to the great and resplendent light of printing. It was necessary, indeed it was necessary, that these writings which speak of Divine illumination be deemed worthy of the light given by printing. Thereby Kyrios Ioannis Mavrogordatos frees from the toil of copying those who know this art, and, at the same time arouses in those who do not the intense love to acquire them and put their teachings into practice.

Thus, very dear reader, you have, through ever excellent Kyrios Ioannis, at small expense, this spiritual publication, which is a treasury of inner wakefulness, a guarding of the mind, a mystical school of mental prayer. This book is an excellent exposition of the practical virtues, an infallible guide of contemplation, a Paradise of the Fathers, the golden series of the virtues. This work is a rich teaching of Jesus, a trumpet that recalls Grace, in a few words, it is the very instrument of theosis, the most desired thing for which we longed for years but could not find.

Therefore, it would be an absolute duty and obligation to entreat God with long prayers for the benefactor and his associates,[1] that they too attain theosis to the same degree; and since they labored for it, to be the first to enjoy the fruits.

At this point, however, someone might interrupt this discourse, saying that it is not proper to publish in this work some things that would be strange to the ears of many, for there is an accompanying danger. To such a person we reply, briefly, that we did not undertake to prepare this work following our own thoughts, but rather the example of others. On the one hand, we follow Holy Scripture, which enjoins all the pious to pray unceasingly and to have always before them the Lord.[2] From the side of the written tradition of the Fathers, St. Basil the Great[3] says that it is impious to say that there is something forbidden or impossible in the Commandments of the Spirit, and Gregory the Theologian gave to all the peoples whom he shepherded the counsel to remember God more often than they breathe. Further, divine Chrysostom wrote three whole sermons con-

---

[1] The term "associates" apparently refers to Sts. Macarios of Corinth and Nicodemos the Hagiorite, who compiled and edited the *Philokalia*.

[2] *1 Thessalonians* 5: 17; *Psalms* 15:8.

[3] *Ca.* 329-379.

cerning unceasing and mental prayer; and in countless places in his other sermons he exhorts all to pray
always. And admirable Gregory the Sinaite,[1] going
about in various cities, taught the salvific practice.

From what we have said, it is evident that this
work presents a practice irreproachable from every
point of view. It would be, therefore, very opportune
to employ the invitation of *Wisdom*[2] for the banquet,
and to invite with a lofty proclamation to the spiritual banquet of this publication all who do not hate
divine banquets, and do not offer as excuses for not
coming to it the fields, the oxen, and the women
mentioned in the Gospel.[3]

Come, therefore, come. Eat of the bread of knowledge and wisdom contained in it. And drink a wine
that spiritually gladdens the heart, and draws attachment to the objects of the bodily senses, owing to the
theosis which that ecstasy produces. And be intoxicated with a really sober intoxication. Come, all who
are participants in the Orthodox call, both laymen
and monks, all who are seeking to find the Kingdom
of God which is within you, and the treasure which
is hidden in the field of your heart. And this treasure

[1] *Ca.* 1265-1346.
[2] *Proverbs* 9:1-6.
[3] *Luke* 14:18-20.

is sweet Jesus Christ. Thus, free from the captivity of this world, and the wandering of your mind, and with your heart purified from the passions, with the unceasing awesome invocation of our Lord Jesus Christ, together with the other cooperating virtues taught by this work, you will be united with one another. And thus united will all be united with God, according to the entreaty of our Lord to His Father, Who said: "that they may be one, as we are one."[1]

Thus united with Him and altogether changed by the ecstasy which is effected by divine eros, may you be abundantly deified, possessing spiritual consciousness and a secure form of knowledge, and return to the original plan of God, glorifying the Father, the Son, and the Holy Spirit. To this transcendently Holy Godhead is proper all glory, honor, and worship unto the ages of ages. Amen.

---

[1] *Luke* 17:21, *Matthew* 13:44.

CHAPTER 1

BRIEF LIFE OF OUR HOLY FATHER
ANTONY THE GREAT
WHOSE MEMORY IS CELEBRATED ON
JANUARY 17

Our great Father Antony, the chief of the choir of ascetics (ἀσκηταί), flourished during the reign of Constantine the Great, about the year 330 A.D.[1] He was a contemporary of Athanasios the Great, who wrote an extended account of his life.

He attained to extreme virtue and freedom from passions. Although he had not learned letters, he had a teacher from Above—the wisdom of the Spirit which bestows understanding upon fishermen and the childlike. His mind, having been illuminated by this wisdom, he presented many holy and spiritual counsels pertaining to various subjects. And he offered exceedingly wise answers to those who asked

[1] According to historians, St. Antony was born in Egypt in 250 and died in 355.

41

him questions. These answers are full of profit for the soul, as is evident in many places in *Books of Elders* (Γεροντικά). Besides them, this man of blessed memory left for us the one hundred and seventy texts contained in the present book.

That these texts are a genuine product of his God-like mind is confirmed by, among others, the Hieromartyr Peter Damascene.[2] The very character of expression, however, also removes all occasion for doubt, and all but speaks out to those who go through them carefully that they belong to that holy, very early, Antiquity.

It is not to be wondered at, therefore, that the language of the texts tends towards the simpler form of a homily and the old-fashioned and plain diction. What is particularly admirable is that through such simplicity there accrues such great salvation and benefit to those who read these texts, their power of persuasion, the delight they evoke, and generally how there bursts forth good character and the strictness of the Evangelical way of life! At all events, those who taste of this honey with the spiritual sense of taste will be delighted.

---

[2] 12th century.

OUR FATHER AMONG THE SAINTS
ANTONY THE GREAT

COUNSELS ON THE CHARACTER OF MEN AND ON THE VIRTUOUS LIFE

In 170 Texts

1. Men (ἄνθρωποι) are improperly called rational (λογικοί); it is not those who have learned thoroughly the discourses and books of the wise men of old that are rational, but those who have a rational soul (λογικὴ ψυχή) and can discern what is good and what is evil, and avoid what is evil and harmful to the soul, but zealously keep, with the aid of practice, what is good and beneficial to the soul, and do this with many thanks to God. These alone should be called truly rational men (λογικοὶ ἄνθρωποι).[3]

---

[3] Cf. the following statements in *St. Antony's Letters* translated by Derwas J. Chitty: "In the case of those rational natures in which the Covenant grew cold, and their intellectual perception died, so that they were no longer able to know themselves according to their first condition, concerning them I say that they became altogether irrational" (Letter II,

SAINT ANTHONY THE GREAT

2. The truly rational man is zealous about one thing: to obey and please the God of all creatures, and to discipline his soul with regard to this: how to do what is acceptable to God, thanking Him for His so benevolent and great providence and government of all things, whatever it may happen to be in the case of his own life. For it is absurd to thank physicians for giving us medicines that are bitter and unpleasant, for the sake of the health of our bodies, but to be ungrateful to God for the things that appear to us harsh, and not to perceive that everything happens to us as is needful and for our benefit, according to His providence. Now knowledge (γνῶσις) of God and faith (πίστις) in Him is the salvation (σωτηρία) and perfection (τελειότης) of the soul.[4]

3. We have received from God self-restraint, forbearance, temperance, perseverance, patience, and

p. 6). "We are called rational, yet have put on the mind of irrational beings" (Letter VI, p. 18). "It behooves us all to exercise our minds and senses to understand the distinction between good and evil" (Letter VII, p. 25). Cf. St. Athanasios the Great: "Saint Antony was governed by reason (λόγος), and was in the state according to nature" (*The Life of Saint Antony*, § 14). Cf. also St. Gregory the Sinaite: "Only those who through their purity have become saints are rational according to nature" (Φιλοκαλία, Vol. IV, Athens, 1961, p. 31).

[4] Cf. the emphasis on faith, salvation, and perfection in the New Testament.

the like, which are great and virtuous powers[5] that oppose and resist difficulties and help us to face them. If we cultivate and use them, and have them at hand, we reckon nothing that happens to us as painful, grievous or unbearable, reflecting that all are human and are overcome by the virtues within us. Those who are foolish in soul do not remember this, for they do not reflect that all things happen to us well and as they ought to for our interest, in order that our virtues might shine and we be crowned by God.

4. If you regard the acquisition of money and its lavish use as only a short-lived fantasy, and realize that the virtuous and God-pleasing way of life is superior to wealth, and steadfastly meditate on this and recall it, you will not groan, or lament, or censure anyone, but will thank God for everything, seeing those who are worse than yourself, basing themselves on repute and money. For lust, love of glory, and ignorance are extremely evil passions of the soul.

5. The rational man (ὁ λογικὸς ἄνθρωπος), examining himself, assays what is appropriate and useful

[5] We have received these as capacities susceptible of development through a life according to God. Cf. Letter II, in Chitty, *St. Antony Letters*, p. 1: "Patriarch Abraham had learned to love God from the law implanted in his nature."

for him, what is proper to the soul and beneficial to it, and what is foreign to it. Thus he avoids what is harmful to the soul being foreign to it and separating him from immortality.

6. The more moderate one's life is the happier one is, for he does not have cares for many things, such as, slaves, farms, and the acquisition of animals. For when we attach ourselves to these, and fall into the vexations that arise from them, we blame God. And through our self-willed desire our spiritual death is induced and we remain wandering about in the darkness of a life of sinful actions, not knowing ourselves.

7. One should not say that it is impossible for man to attain a virtuous life, but that it is not easy, and is not easily understood by chance persons. Now those men partake of the virtuous life who are pious and have a God-loving mind (νοῦς); for the ordinary mind is worldly (κοσμικός) and changing. It produces both good and evil thoughts, changes in nature, and turns towards material things (τὴν ὕλην). The God-loving mind, on the other hand, opposes the badness which arises in men from their sloth.

8. Those who lack culture regard discourses as ridiculous and do not want to hear them, because their lack of culture is exposed, and they want all to be like

themselves. In the same manner, those who are intemperate in their life and ways want all others to be worse than themselves, thinking that they will attain blamelessness for themselves through the abounding of badness of others. The weak soul is confused and perishes by wickedness, having within itself profligacy, pride, insatiate desire, wrath, rashness, fury, cowardice, disease, hatred, censure, weakness, going astray, ignorance, deception, forgetting God. Through these and the like the wretched soul is punished; it is separated from God.

9. Those who wish to practice the virtuous, devout, and spiritually glorious mode of life should not be judged by affected manners or sham conduct. Like skilled painters and sculptors, it is by their works that they display their virtuous and God-loving way of life. And they shun all evil pleasures as snares (παγίδας).[6]

10. For those who think rightly, the man who is rich and of noble rank, but lacks discipline of the soul and virtue in life, is wretched, just as he who chances to be poor or a slave but is adorned (κεκοσμημένος)

[6] This statement brings to mind the following anecdote: "Abba Antony said: 'I saw all the snares of the Devil spread on the ground, and I sighed and said: Who, then, can escape from them? And I heard a voice saying: Humility" (*The Evergetinos*, Vol. I, Athens, 1953, p. 395).

with discipline of the soul and virtue in life is happy. And just as strangers wander about on the roads, so those who do not concern themselves with the virtuous life, being led astray by lower desires, perish.

11. He ought to be called a maker-of-men (ἀνθρωποποιός) who is able to tame undisciplined men, so that they will love discourses and discipline. Similarly, they ought to be called makers-of-men who change those who lead an intemperate life, so that they live in a virtuous and God-pleasing manner, inasmuch as they regenerate these men. For meekness (πραότης)[7] and self-restraint are happiness and good hope (ἐλπίς) for the souls of men.[8]

12. Men ought in reality and properly to discipline their manners and way of life. When this is achieved, what pertains to God is easily learned. For he who reveres God with all his heart[9] and with faith[10] receives provision from Him to control his anger and desire—for desire and anger are the cause of all evils.

---

[7] Cf. Christ: "Blessed are the meek" (*Matthew* 5: 5).

[8] Mention was made earlier (§ 2) of the Christian virtue of faith; here, reference is made to another Christian virtue, hope; later, reference is made to love, the highest of the three virtues.

[9] Cf. Christ: "Thou shall love the Lord thy God with all thy heart, and with all thy soul, and with all the mind" (*Matthew* 22: 37).

[10] Cf. Christ: "Have faith in God" (*Mark* 11: 22).

13. He is called a man (ἄνθρωπος) who either is in actuality rational or is susceptible of being corrected. He who is incorrigible is called inhuman (ἀπάνθρωπος), for this is a characteristic of those who are inhuman. Such men should be avoided, because it is not possible for those who live together with vice ever to be among the immortal.[11]

14. When the rational faculty (τὸ λογικόν) is truly present in us, it makes us worthy of being called human beings. When we lack it we differ from the irrational animals only in the form of our bodily members and in our voice. Let therefore the well-disposed man realize that he is immortal, and he will hate all shameful desires, which are the cause of spiritual death to men.

15. Just as every art shows its excellence in the ordering of its subject-matter, as for instance one man works on timber, another on copper, another on gold and silver, so we who hear of the good life and of the virtuous and God-pleasing conduct, ought to be manifestly truly rational in soul, and not in the form of the body alone. Now the truly rational and God-loving soul knows directly the things in life, and rec-

[11] Cf. *Psalm* 17: 25-26: "With the holy man thou wilt be holy; and with the innocent man thou wilt be innocent. And with the excellent man thou wilt be excellent; and with the perverse man thou wilt be perverse."

onciles itself lovingly with God, and sincerely thanks Him, having all its aspiration and mind directed towards Him.[12]

16. Just as helmsmen steer the ship in the proper direction in order to avoid hitting a reef or shoal, so let those who aspire after the virtuous life consider carefully what they ought to do and what they ought to avoid. And let them regard the true and Divine Laws as being for their interest, cutting off the evil thoughts of the soul.

17. Just as helmsmen and charioteers attain their goal by attention and diligence, so must those who strive after the right and virtuous life exercise attention and take thought how to live as they ought and in a manner that is pleasing to God. For he who wants it, and has perceived that he has the capability to attain it, by faith (πιστεύων) rises to incorruptibility.

18. Let not those be regarded by you as free (ἐλεύθεροι) who chance to be freemen, but those who are free in their life and ways. For one should not call truly free those rulers who are wicked or intemperate, for they are slaves of earthly passions, whereas freedom and happiness of the soul consist in genu-

---

[12] Cf. *Matthew* 22: 37: "Thou shalt love God with all thy heart, and with all thy soul, and with all thy mind."

ine purity (καθαρότης)[13] and contempt of transitory things (τῶν προσκαίρων καταφρόνησις).[14]

19. Remind yourself that you must unceasingly exhibit yourself through your good way of life and your good deeds themselves. For it is thus also that the sick find and recognize physicians as benefactors and saviors—not through their words, but through their deeds.

20. A truly rational and virtuous soul is recognized from a man's look, walk, voice, laughter, manner of spending his time, and the circumstances of his life.[15] Everything in such a soul has been thoroughly changed and corrected so as to become graceful. For its God-loving rational faculty, being a vigilant gate-keeper (ὁ νοῦς πυλωρὸς νηφάλιος ὑπάρχων) bars entry to evil and ugly thoughts.[16]

---

[13] Cf. *Hebrews* 9: 13.

[14] Cf. *2 Corinthians* 4: 18: "We look not at the things which are seen, but at the things which are not seen; for the things which are seen are temporal (πρόσκαιρα), but the things which are not seen are eternal."

[15] Cf. *Wisdom of Sirach*: "The dress of a man, his laughter, and his manner of walking announce his character" (Septuagint, 19:30).

[16] Cf. Hesychios the Presbyter: "Inner watchfulness (νῆψις) is the steadfast standing of the mind at the gate of the heart, watching the thoughts that are coming as thieves" (Φιλοκαλία, Vol. I, Athens, 1960, p. 142). The word νηφάλιος is used in St. Paul's *First Epistle to Timothy* (3: 2)

21. Examine the things that pertain to you, and prove for yourself that rulers and masters have authority only over the body, not over the soul;[17] and let this always be before your mind. Wherefore, whether they command murders or other foul, unjust, and soul-corrupting acts, you must not obey them, even if they torture your body. For God created the soul with the power of free-choice-and-self-control (τὸ αὐτεξούσιον), of doing good or doing evil.

22. The rational soul endeavors to free itself from the paths of conceit, arrogance, deception, envy, avarice, and the like, which are works of the demons[18] and of evil choice. All this is successfully achieved through persistent zeal and practice by a man whose desire is not directed towards the pleasures.

23. Those who lead a life of privation and not one of abundance deliver themselves from dangers and have no need of protectors. By overcoming desire in all things, they easily find the path that leads to God.

24. Rational men have no need to pay attention (προσέχειν) to many conversations, but only to those which are profitable, which are guided by

and his *Epistle to Titus* (2: 2).

[17] Cf. Christ: "Fear not them which kill the body, but are not able to kill the soul" (*Matthew* 10: 28).

[18] Cf. *Luke* 8: 12, *John*, 8: 44.

God's will. For thus men come again to life and the Eternal Light (φῶς αἰώνιον).[19]

25. Those who seek to lead a life that is virtuous and pleasing to God must free themselves from conceit and all empty and false glory, and should endeavor to correct their life and mind. For a God-loving and steadfast mind is an ascent and way to God.

26. There is no profit in learning discourses, if there is no life of the soul that is acceptable and pleasing to God. The cause of all evils is delusion, deception, and ignorance of God.[20]

27. Meditation (μελέτη) on the most beautiful life (κάλλιστος βίος)[21] and care of the soul render men good and God-loving. For he who seeks God finds Him by overcoming desire in all things, not shrinking from prayer (εὐχή). Such a man does not fear demons.

28. Those who are deceived by worldly (βιωτικαί)[22]

[19] Cf. *John*: "In Him was Life; and the Life was the Light of men. And the Light shineth in darkness; and the darkness comprehended it not" (1: 4-5).

[20] Cf. Christ: "And ye shall know the Truth, and the Truth shall make you free" (*John* 8: 32). Cf. St. Paul: "Awake to righteousness, and sin not; for some have not the knowledge of God: I speak this to your shame" (*1 Corinthians* 15: 34).

[21] This expression fits with the naming of the book *Philokalia*, which means "love of the beautiful."

[22] Cf. *Luke*, 21: 34: "Take heed to yourselves, lest at any time your hearts be overcharged with surfeiting, and drunken-

hopes and know the things that must be done for the most beautiful life (κάλλιστος βίος) only so far as words go, are in the same state as those who are furnished with medicines and medical instruments but neither know how to use them, nor take the trouble to learn. Therefore, we must never blame our birth nor anyone else but ourselves as the cause of our sinful actions; for if the soul chooses to be in a state of indolence, it cannot remain invincible.

29. He who does not know how to distinguish what is good and what is evil cannot judge who is good and who is evil. He who knows God is good. If one is not good, he knows nothing about God and never will know; for goodness is the way to God.

30. Good and God-loving men reprove others with regard to evil when they are present. When they are not present they neither censure them, nor let others say something in the way of censure when they attempt.

31. In conversations all harshness should be avoided; for modesty and temperance are able to *adorn* (κοσμεῖν)[23] rational men even more than virgins. A God-loving mind is a light which illumines the soul, just as the sun illumines the body.

ness, and worldly cares (μερίμναις βιωτικαῖς)."
[23] κοσμεῖν -- *explain*

32. With regard to every passion that arises in your soul, remember that those who think rightly, and want to put what belongs to them in its proper and safe place, consider as pleasant not the acquisition of perishing things, but true and sound beliefs. It is these that render them happy. For wealth is seized and carried off by the more powerful, whereas virtue of the soul is the only acquisition which is safe and cannot be carried off, and which saves after death those who possess it. The fantasies about wealth and about other pleasures do not delude those who think in this manner.

33. Those who are inconstant and uninstructed should not make trial of reasonable men. Now a reasonable man is one who pleases God and for the most part remains silent, saying few things, only what is necessary and pleasing to God.

34. Those who pursue a virtuous and God-pleasing life cultivate the virtues of the soul, as being their own possession and eternal delight, and they enjoy transitory things only so far as conditions permit and God wills and bestows them. They use them quite gladly and gratefully, even though they happen to be altogether moderate. For sumptuous meals nourish bodies, inasmuch as they are material, but knowledge of God, self-restraint, goodness, beneficence,

piety, and meekness (πραότης)[24] deify (ἀποθεοί) the soul.[25]

35. Rulers who attempt to constrain men to undertake foul and soul-corrupting acts do not succeed. For the soul has been created with the power of free choice and self-control. They fetter the body, but not the power of choice, of which the rational man is the master through God, Who created man and is more powerful than all authority, force, and power.

36. Let those who consider it a misfortune to lose money, or children, or slaves, or anything else that belongs to them, realize that they should be satisfied with what is given to them by God. And when it is necessary to return these, they should do so readily and gratefully, not being bitter over the deprivation of them, or rather the return of them—for having used what was not their own, they returned it.

37. It is the part of the good man not to sell his free opinion by having his eye turned to the acquisition of money, even if it should happen that much is offered to him. For worldly things (τὰ βιωτικά)[26] are as in a dream, and the fantasies of wealth are obscure and of brief duration.

---

[24] Cf. *Matthew* 5: 5: "Blessed are the meek."

[25] Here we have the Orthodox concept of *theosis*.

[26] Cf. an earlier use of this Scriptural term, text 28.

38. Let those who are truly men endeavor to live in such a God-loving and virtuous manner that their virtuous life will shine amongst other men,[27] just as a small purple stripe, when put on white clothes, adorns them and makes them shine and be noticed. They thus prompt others to cultivate the virtues of the soul with greater steadfastness.

39. Sensible men must examine well their strength and the power of the virtues of the soul which are present in them, and thus prepare themselves and oppose the passions they encounter, according to the strength which they possess, which has been naturally granted to them by God. In relation to carnal beauty and every desire that is harmful to the soul there is self-restraint; in relation to pains and want there is patient endurance; in relation to reproach and anger, there is forbearance; and so on.

40. It is impossible for one to become good and wise suddenly. One becomes such through painstaking practice, his mode of life, experience, time, askesis (ἄσκησις) and the desire for virtuous deeds. The good and God-loving man, who truly knows God, does not cease doing abundantly all that is pleasing

[27] Cf. Christ: "Let your light so shine before men, that they may see your good works and glorify your Father Who is in Heaven" (*Matthew* 5: 16).

to God. Such men are rare.

41. Men with little natural talent should not de-spair of themselves and become indolent as regards the God-loving and virtuous life, and despise it as unattainable, beyond their reach. Instead, they should exercise their capacity and take care of them-selves. For even if they be unable to attain the limit with respect to virtue and salvation, through prac-tice (μελέτη) and aspiration they will become better or at least will not become worse—which is no small profit for the soul.

42. Through the rational faculty man is connected with the ineffable and Divine power; and through his bodily nature he has kinship with the animals. Few men, those who are perfect (τέλειοι)[28] and ratio-nal, endeavor to have their thoughts turned towards God the Savior (Θεὸν καὶ Σωτῆρα),[29] and strive to have kinship with Him. This they manifest through their deeds and virtuous way of life. But most men, those who are foolish in soul, having abandoned that divine and immortal adoption as sons of God,[30] inclin-ing towards the mortal, unfortunate, and short-lived

[28] Cf. *Matthew* 5: 48: "ἔσεσθε τέλειοι".
[29] Cf. *Luke* 1: 47: "And my spirit hath rejoiced in God my Savior."
[30] Cf. St. Paul: "For as many as are led by the Spirit of God, they are sons of God" (*Romans* 8: 14; cf. *Romans* 8: 23).

kinship with the body, and being concerned like the irrational animals with the things of the flesh, and inflamed with pleasures, separate themselves from God, and drag down the soul from Heaven to the abyss through their bad wishes.

43. The rational man, being concerned with communion with the divine and union with it, will never fall in love with anything earthly or base, but has his mind turned towards the heavenly and eternal. And he knows that this is the will of God: that man be saved, this will being the cause of all things beautiful (καλά)[31] and the source of the eternal good things (ἀγαθά) for men.[32]

44. When you find someone arguing and fighting against the truth and what is obvious, leaving the disputation, withdraw from such a man, since his intellect has been petrified. For just as very foul water renders good wines useless, so bad conversations corrupt those who are virtuous in life and mind.[33]

45. If we make every effort and use every means in order to avoid bodily death, much more should

---

[31] Cf. texts 27 and 28 above: "ὁ κάλλιστος βίος".

[32] Cf. St. Paul: "But Christ being come a high priest of good things..." (*Hebrews* 9: 11).

[33] Cf. St. Paul: "A man that is a heretic, after the first and second admonition reject" (*Titus* 3: 10); "Evil associations corrupt good morals" (*1 Corinthians* 15: 33).

we endeavor to avoid death of the soul. For there is no obstacle for him who wants to be saved, except negligence and sloth of the soul.

46. Those who are disinclined to take notice of what is to their interest, and what is well said, are regarded as being in a bad state. Those, on the other hand, who perceive the truth, but quarrel shamelessly, are dead in their rational faculty, and their behavior has become bestialized. They do not know God and their soul has not been illumined.

47. God has produced the various species of animals for our needs through His Logos (Λόγος).[34] Some he created to be eaten, others to serve us. And He created man to be a spectator of them and of their actions, and as their grateful interpreter. Wherefore, let men strive lest they die without seeing and apprehending God and His works, like the irrational animals. Man ought to know that God is omnipotent, and that there is nothing that can oppose Him Who is omnipotent.[35] He creates out of nothing[36] all things that He wills, by His Logos, for the salvation

[34] Cf. *John* 1: 1, 2: "In the beginning was the Logos, and the Logos was with God, and the Logos was God... All things were made by Him."

[35] Cf. Christ: "With God all things are possible" (*Matthew* 20: 26).

[36] A basic Christian doctrine.

of men.

48. The beings in Heaven are immortal through the goodness in them, whereas the beings on the Earth become mortal because of the self-willed evil in them, which arises in the foolish from their sloth and ignorance of God.

49. Death, when understood by men, is immortality;[37] but not being understood by the ignorant it is death. This death should not be feared; what should be feared is the perdition of the soul, which is ignorance of God; for this is terrible for the soul.

50. Badness (κακία) is an affection of matter; hence it is not possible for a body to come into being free of badness. The rational soul, perceiving this, shakes off the heaviness of matter, which is badness, and emerging from this weight, it comes to know the God of all beings, and watches the body as an enemy, not yielding to it.[38] Thus the soul is crowned by God for having conquered the passions of badness and of matter.[39]

---

[37] Cf. St. Paul: "When this mortal shall have put on immortality, then shall be brought to pass the saying that is written: Death is swallowed up in victory" (*1 Corinthians* 15: 54).

[38] Cf. St. Paul: "I keep under my body and bring it into subjection: lest that by any means, when I have preached to others, I myself should be a castaway" (*1 Corinthians* 9: 27).

[39] Cf. Letter VI of St. Antony (in Chitty, *St. Antony's Letters*):

51. When badness has come to be known by the soul, it is hated by the soul as a most foul beast. When badness remains unknown, it is loved by him who is ignorant about it. And it has him as a captive, treating him as a slave. Such an unfortunate and wretched man neither sees his true interest nor knows it, but thinks he is adorned by badness and rejoices.

52. The pure soul, being good, is illumined and made resplendent by God. And then the mind (νοῦς) apprehends what is good and begets thoughts that are dear to God. When, however, the soul is defiled by badness, and God turns away from it, or rather the soul separates itself from God, evil demons approach it and come into the mind and suggest (ὑπβάλλουσι) unholy acts to the soul: adulteries, murders, robberies, sacrileges, and the like—whatever things are acts of demons.[40]

"Therefore, while we are still clothed in *this heavy body*, let us rouse up God in ourselves... Strive to offer yourselves as a sacrifice to God always—and give gladness ... to all the band of the saints, and to me also, this poor wretch, who am dwelling in *this house of clay and darkness*" (pp. 20-21). What is said here and above is to be understood in terms of *levels* of reality. The body represents a lower level of reality than the soul. The body is gross, "heavy,"

[40] That demons act on the soul, particularly on the imagination, by means of suggestion, telepathically, is a view that appears in other texts of St. Antony (e.g. 89, 96), and often elsewhere in the *Philokalia*.

53. Those who know God are filled with every good impulse. And desiring heavenly things, they despise worldly things (τὰ βιωτικά). Such men are neither pleasing to many people, nor are pleased by many. As a result, they are not only hated, but also ridiculed by many of the foolish. And they are content to suffer everything from want, knowing that the things which appear to the many as evil are really good. For he who apprehends heavenly things (τὰ οὐράνια) believes in God, knowing that all are creatures of His will. On the other hand, he who does not apprehend heavenly things never believes that the world is a work of God and was made for the salvation of man.

54. Those who are full of badness and are drunken with ignorance do not know God, and are not awake (οὐδὲ νήφουσι) in soul.[41] God is spiritual (νοητός); and though not visible, is very manifest in visible things,[42] as is the soul in the body. And if it is impossible for the body to be formed without a soul, so it is impossible for any of the things which are visible and exist to be formed without God.[43]

[41] The Orthodox practice of inner wakefulness or watchfulness (νῆψις) is alluded to.
[42] Cf. *Romans* 1: 20: "The invisible things of God are clearly seen, being understood by the things that are made."
[43] Cf. *St. John* 1: 3: "All things were made by Him: and

55. Why was man created? In order that by observing well the creatures of God he might see and glorify Him Who created them for the sake of man. The mind (νοῦς) that is purified is lovable to God. It is an invisible good, which is given by God to those who are worthy through their good way of life.

56. He is free who is not a slave to pleasures, but through wisdom and temperance masters the body, is satisfied with what is given to him by God, and is very grateful to Him, even though this might happen to be altogether moderate. If the God-loving mind and soul are in harmony, the whole body is calm, even if unwillingly. For when the soul wants, every carnal desire is extinguished.

57. Those who are not content with what they have for living enslave themselves to passions that disturb the soul, and suggest to it thoughts and fantasies that the good things which they have are bad. And just as tunics that are oversized hinder those who are competing in a race, in the same manner the desire for abundance that is beyond measure does not allow souls to struggle or to be saved.

58. In whatever state an individual finds himself unwillingly and against his wish, that for him is a prison and punishment. Hence, be content with the

without Him was not any thing made that was made."

things that you have now, lest having them without gratitude you punish yourself through your insensibility. There is one path to this, that of despising worldly things (τὰ βιωτικά).

59. Just as we have the sense of sight from God in order that we might gain knowledge of visible things: what white is, what the color of ink is, and so on, similarly, the rational faculty (τὸ λογικόν) has been given to us by God in order that we may distinguish what is good for the soul. Desire, detached from reason, generates pleasure and does not allow the soul to be saved or to attain union with God (τῷ Θεῷ συναφθῆναι).[44]

60. Sinful acts are not those which are according to nature, but are evil acts of deliberate choice. It is not a sin to eat; what is a sin is not to eat with gratitude and in an orderly and self-restrained manner, so that the body might be sustained in life unaffected by evil thoughts. Nor is it a sin to look chastely; what is a sin is to look with envy, pride, and greed; and not to listen peacefully, but angrily; and not to guide the tongue as with a bit and bridle towards thanks and prayer (προσευχή), but to speak ill of others; and not to employ the hands for charity, but for murders and robberies. In such ways every part of the body sins,

---

[44] One more reference to *theosis*.

performing of one's own choice acts that are evil, contrary to the will of God.

61. If you doubt that each of the acts performed is observed by God, consider that although you are a human being and dust, you can at the same time watch and apprehend manifold places, how much more God, Who sees all things like a grain of mustard seed (κόκκος σινάπεως),[45] Who vivifies and sustains all creatures as He wills.

62. When you close the doors of your dwelling-place and are alone, know that there is present with you the Angel (Ἄγγελος)[46] whom God has appointed for each man, whom the Greeks call one's personal genius. This Angel, being sleepless and not to be deceived, is always present with you, seeing all things and not being hindered by darkness; and that along with him is God, too, in every place. For there is no place or matter (ὕλη) where God is not, being greater than all things and containing all in His hand.[47]

63. If soldiers remain faithful to Caesar because

---

[45] Cf. *Matthew* 17: 20: "As a grain of mustard seed."

[46] Cf. The epiclesis in the Divine Liturgy: "For an Angel of peace, a faithful guide, a guardian of our souls and bodies, let us ask the Lord."

[47] Cf. St. Peter: "Humble yourselves, therefore, under the mighty hand of God, that He may exalt you in due time" (*1 Peter* 5: 6).

the foods are provided by him, how much more
ought we to endeavor to thank God unceasingly
(ἀδιαλείπτως),[48] with never silent lips, and to praise
Him Who created all things for the sake of man?

64. Gratitude to God and a virtuous way of life are
fruits that please God. The fruits of the earth are not
brought to perfection in an hour, but by time and
rain and care. Similarly, the fruits of men become
bright through askesis (ἄσκησις), study, time, perseverance, self-restraint, and patience. And if because
of these you should ever appear to some to be pious,
distrust yourself, so long as you are in the body, and
think that nothing of yours pleases God. For know
that it is not easy for man to keep himself sinless until the end.

65. There is nothing more precious among men
than speech. So powerful is speech, that it is by
speech and thanks that we worship God, and by unprofitable or slanderous speech that we condemn
our soul. It is characteristic of an insensible man to
throw the blame for his sinning on his descent or
on something else, using evil speech or deeds of his
own free choice.

[48] Cf. St. Paul: "We give thanks to God always" (1
Thessalonians 1: 2: "We thank God without ceasing" (1
Thessalonians 2: 13); "Pray without ceasing" (1 Thessalonians
5: 17).

66. If we endeavor to cure the passions of the body because of the ridicule of chance persons, much more is there every need for us to endeavor to cure the passions of the soul—inasmuch as we will be judged facing God—lest we be found dishonored and ridiculous. For having the power of free will (αὐτεξούσιον), if we wish, when we desire evil actions, we are able to avoid performing them. And it is in our power to live in a manner that is pleasing to God. And no one will ever force us, when we are unwilling, to do what is evil. Struggling thus, we shall be persons worthy of God, living as Angels in the Heavens.[49]

67. If you wish, you are a slave of the passions; if you wish, you are free and do not yield to the passions. God created you with the power of free choice and self-control; and he who overcomes the passions of the flesh is crowned with incorruption. For if there were no passions, there would have been no virtues, nor would there be crowns awarded by God to those who are worthy.

68. Individuals who do not see what is to their interest and good are blind in soul, and their power

[49] Reference to Angels appears in earlier texts, too, e.g. § 62. Here and elsewhere St. Antony uses the plural form of heaven: "Heavens." This is consistent with diction (as in the Lord's Prayer) of the orginal, Greek New Testament.

of discernment (τὸ διακριτικόν)[50] has grown dull. Hence, the mind must not pay attention (προσέχειν) to them, lest we also necessarily fall imprudently into the same faults, having become blind.

69. We should not become angry with those who sin, even if the things they do are grounds for complaint deserving punishment. Instead, for the sake of what is right in itself, we ought to cause those who stumble to repent. And if need be, we should chastize them ourselves, or have them chastised by others. We should not become angry or excited, because anger acts only according to passion and not according to judgment and what is right. Wherefore, neither must we approve of those who show mercy more than is proper. The wicked must be punished for the sake of what is good and just, and not because we are moved by our passion of anger.

70. The possession of the soul is alone one that is safe and inviolate. It consists in a way of life that is virtuous and pleasing to God, and in knowledge and performing good deeds. Wealth is a blind guide and a foolish counselor; and he who uses wealth in an evil and self-indulgent manner loses his foolish soul.[51]

[50] St. John Cassian has a long discussion on discernment. He regards it as the highest of the virtues. See the Greek *Philokalia*, Volume I, Athens, 1957, p. 84 ff.

[51] Cf. *Matthew* 16: 26: "What is a man profited, if he shall

71. Men must either not acquire anything super-fluous, or if they possess something that is superflu-ous they must realize with certainty that all things in this life are by nature perishable, easy to disperse, capable of being lost and broken. And they ought not to think lightly of what happens.

72. Know that the sufferings of the body are natu-rally proper to the body, inasmuch as it is corruptible and material (ὑλικόν). It is necessary, therefore, that the disciplined soul gratefully put forth patient endur-ance and perseverance in relation to such sufferings, and not to blame God for having created the body.

73. Those who compete at the Olympic Games are not crowned after achieving victory over the first opponent, or the second, or the third, but after they have defeated all those who have competed against them. Similarly, therefore, each individual who wishes to be crowned by God must discipline his soul to exercise self-control not only in relation to the body, but also in relation to profits, robberies, envy, foods, empty glory, reproaches, death, and all such things.[52]

gain the whole world and lose his own soul?"

[52] Cf. St. Paul: "Know ye not that they who run in a race run all, but one receiveth the prize? So run, that ye may obtain. And every man that striveth for the mastery is temperate in all things. Now they do it to obtain a corruptible crown: but

74. Let us not pursue for the sake of human praise the way of life that is good and loved by God. Let us instead pursue the virtuous life for the sake of the salvation of our soul; for death is daily before our eyes and human things are uncertain.

75. It is in our power to live with self-control, but it is not in our power to become wealthy. What, then? Is it necessary to condemn our soul through the short-lived fantasies of wealth, which is not in our power to acquire? Should we merely desire wealth? Oh! How foolishly we behave, not knowing that before all the virtues is humility,[53] just as before all the passions is gluttony and the desire for worldly things.

76. Prudent men (ἔμφρονες) unceasingly remember that by enduring small and short-lived sufferings in life, men enjoy the greatest pleasure and eternal bliss after death. Wherefore, if he who struggles against the passions and wishes to be crowned by God, should fall, he should not faint and remain fallen, and despair of himself, but should arise and struggle again and take thought to be saved. Until his last breath he should keep rising from the falls

we an incorruptible" (*1 Corinthians* 9: 24-25).

[53] Cf. St. Gregory Palamas: "Humility is the begetter and sustainer of all the virtues" (Φιλοκαλία, Vol. 4, Athens, 1961, p. 109).

that occur.[54] For persistent efforts are weapons of the virtues and conducive to the salvation of the soul.

77. The circumstances of life cause worthy men and spiritual athletes to be crowned by God. Therefore, they must in the present life make themselves dead to all worldly things (τὰ βιωτικά).[55] For a dead man never takes thought for anything worldly.

78. The rational and struggling soul must not cower and be timid towards the passions that arise, and be derided as being cowardly. For the soul, being disturbed by fantasies of worldly things, departs from what is proper. The virtues of the soul precede the eternal blessings, while the self-willed vices of men become the causes of punishments.

79. Rational man is combated by the mental senses (τὰς λογικὰς αἰσθήσεις) in him through the passions of the soul. The bodily senses (αἱ τοῦ σώματος αἰσθήσεις) are five: sight, smell, hearing, taste, and touch. Through these five senses the wretched soul, becoming subject to its four passions, is taken

[54] Cf. St. John Climacos: "Do not be surprised that you fall every day; do not give up, but stand your ground courageously. And assuredly the Angel who guards you will honor your patience....With God all things are possible" (*The Ladder of Divine Ascent*, Boston, 1991, Step 5, text 30).

[55] Cf. *Colossians* 3: 5: "Mortify therefore fornication, uncleanliness, inordinate affection, evil concupiscence, and covetousness."

captive. The four passions of the soul are vainglory, sensual pleasure, anger, and timidity. When a man, having through moral wisdom and reflection acted like a good general, prevails over the passions and conquers them, he is no longer combated. His soul is at peace and is crowned by God, because it has conquered.

80. Of those who come to an inn, some receive beds; others, not having a bed, but sleeping on the ground, sleep no less than those who sleep on beds and snore. And having remained at the inn for the duration of the night, early the next day they leave the beds of the inn and all in common go out carrying only their own belongings. In the same way, both those who have lived moderately well off and those who have lived in glory and wealth, go out of this life as from an inn, taking with them nothing from the luxury and wealth of life, but only their own deeds, either good or bad, which they performed in their lifetime.

81. If you are in a position of superior authority, do not recklessly threaten someone with death, knowing that you too, by nature, are subject to death, and that at death the soul takes off the body like the last tunic (χιτῶνα).[56] Knowing this clearly, exercise meek-

[56] Cf. St. John Chrysostom: "What then, I pray you, is

ness (πραότης) and doing good, and continually thank God. For he who does not have compassion has no virtue in himself.

82. To escape death is impossible and inconceivable. Knowing this, those who are truly rational, and disciplined in the virtues, and in thinking which is pleasing to God, accept death without groans, fear, and mourning. They consider its inexorableness and that it delivers one from the evils of this life.

83. We must not hate those who have forgotten the way of life which is good and pleasing to God, and who do not pay regard to the dogmas (δόγματα) which are true and dear to Him. Rather, we ought to show mercy to them as disabled in the power of discernment, and blind in heart and intellect. For by accepting evil as good they are destroyed by ignorance. And they do not know God, these thrice-wretched and foolish ones in soul.

84. Do not address your words about piety (εὐσέβεια) and right living to the rabble. I do not say this out of malice, but because I think that you will seem ridiculous to those who are thoughtless.

death? Just what it is to put off a garment (ἱμάτιον). For the body is about the soul as a garment; and after laying this aside by means of death, we shall resume it again with the more splendor" (*A Select Library of Nicene and Post-Nicene Fathers*, Vol. IX, p. 374.)

For like rejoices in like, and such discourses find few listeners—perhaps exceedingly rare. It is better not to discourse to such persons, and it is not what God wants for their salvation.

85. The soul suffers with the body, but the body does not suffer with the soul. Thus, when the body is cut, the soul suffers, too. And when the body is vigorous and healthy, the emotions of the soul rejoice together with it. However, when the soul is thinking the body does not think but is left by itself. For thinking is an affection of the soul alone, as are ignorance, pride, unbelief, greed, hatred, envy, anger, contempt, vanity, discord, as well as the perception of goodness. All these are effected by the soul.

86. Reflecting on the attributes of God, be pious, free from envy, good, temperate, meek, forgiving as far as you can, sociable, not quarrelsome, and the like. For this is the inviolate possession of the soul: to please God through such qualities and to judge no one,[57] and to say about no one that so-and-so is wicked and has sinned. It is better to look for one's own faults, to observe one's own conduct, and to see whether it is pleasing to God. For what concern is it

[57] Cf. Christ: "Judge not, that ye be not judged.... And why beholdest thou the mote that is in thy brother's eye, but considerest not the beam that is in thine own eye?" (*Matthew* 7: 1, 3).

to us if another man is wicked?

87. He who is truly a man endeavors to be pious (εὐσεβής). And he is pious who does not desire alien things. Alien things to man are all transitory created things. Therefore, he despises them all, as he is an image of God (εἰκὼν τοῦ Θεοῦ).[58] A man is an image of God when he orders his life rightly and agreeably to God. This is impossible unless a man detaches himself from worldly things (τὰ βιωτικά). Now he who has a God-loving mind (νοῦς) has knowledge of everything profitable to the soul that is engendered by that mind. The God-loving man blames no one else for the sins that he himself commits. This is a mark of a soul that is on the way to salvation.

88. Those who violently endeavor to acquire transitory possessions also love the works of vice. They ignore death and the loss of their own soul,[59] and do not consider what is to their true interest. They do not reflect on what men suffer from wickedness after death.

89. Badness is an affection of matter. God is not the cause of badness. He gave to men knowledge, understanding, the power of discriminating between good and evil, and the power of free-choice-and-

[58] Cf. *Genesis*: "And God said, Let us make man in our image" (1: 26). This is a core Christian doctrine.

[59] Cf. Christ: "What is a man profited, if he shall gain the whole world, and lose his own soul?" (*Matthew* 16: 26).

self-control (τὸ αὐτεξούσιον). What gives birth to the passions of badness is negligence and sloth. God is not at all their cause. The demons have become evil as a result of their own free choice. The same is true of men.[60]

90. The man who lives with piety does not allow wickedness to slip into his soul. When wickedness is absent, the soul is free from what is dangerous and harmful. Such men are neither under the sway of mischievous demons nor under the power of fate. God delivers them from evils and they live unharmed, protected as godlike. If someone praises them, they laugh at him within themselves; while if someone censures them, they do not defend themselves, or become indignant at what such a person says.

91. Evil follows closely nature, just as verdigris follows closely copper, and dirt the body. However, neither the coppersmith made the verdigris, nor one's parents the dirt. Similarly, neither did God create wickedness. God gave to man knowledge and discernment (γνῶσις καὶ διάκρισις), in order that he might avoid evil, knowing that he is harmed by it and is punished. Therefore, watch steadily lest when

[60] Cf. St. John Damascene: "By his free choice the Devil turned from what was according to nature to what is against it; he abandoned good and became evil" (*An Exact Exposition of the Orthodox Faith*, Book Two, chapter 4).

you see someone who is well off in power and wealth you deem him happy, being deceived by a demon through the imagination (φαντασθείς). Instead, let death appear at once before your eyes, and never desire any evil or worldly thing.

92. Our God has granted immortality to those in Heaven. For those on earth He established change. To the universe He gave life and movement. He made everything for man.[61] Therefore, let not the worldly fantasy of a demon who suggests (ὑποβάλλοντος) evil thoughts to your soul carry you away. Instead, reflecting at once on heavenly things, say to yourself: If I wish, it is in my power to be victorious in this struggle (ἀγῶνα) too, against passion, but I will not be victorious if I wish to satisfy my desire. Engage, then, in this struggle which is able to save your soul.

93. Life is the union and conjunction of the mind, the soul, and the body. Death, on the other hand, is not the destruction of these conjoined things, but the dissolution of their union. For by God all are preserved after the dissolution, too.

94. The mind (νοῦς) is not a soul (ψυχή), but a gift

[61] Cf. St. Symeon the New Theologian: "It was for man that the whole of creation was made by God" (*Ta Hapanta tou Hosiou Symeon tou Neou Theologou*, Syros, 1886. p. 31).

of God that saves the soul. A mind that is pleasing to God runs in advances and counsels the soul to despise transitory, material, and corruptible things, and to love ardently eternal, incorruptible, and immaterial (ἄϋλα) goods, and to walk as a man in a body, while through the mind to apprehend and contemplate the things in the Heavens and Divine, and all things together. The God-loving mind is a benefactor of the human soul and its salvation.

95. When the soul is under the sway of the body, it is darkened by pain and pleasure, and undermined. Pain and pleasure are the bad humors of the body. A God-loving mind, acting in opposition, grieves the body and saves the soul, like a physician who cuts and cauterizes bodies.

96. All those souls which are not guided by the rational faculty and governed by it, so that it checks and restrains and governs their passions, that is, pain and pleasure, perish like the irrational animals, their rational faculty being dragged down by the passions, like a charioteer who is overcome by his horses.[62]

97. The greatest disease of the soul, its ruin and perdition, is not to know God, Who created all things

---

[62] Cf. St. Macarios the Egyptian: "The mind (νοῦς) is the charioteer of the soul and harnesses the chariot of the soul, holding the reins of its thoughts" (Ὁμιλίαι Πνευματικαί, Volos, 1954, p. 191).

for man and gave him intuitive and discursive reason, through which, soaring upward, man attains union with God, knows and glorifies Him.

98. The soul is in the body, while in the soul is the mind, and in the mind is discursive reason. Through these, God, being apprehended and glorified, grants to it incorruptibility and eternal bliss. For God has granted being to all existing things solely through His goodness.

99. God, being free of envy, and being good, created man with the power of free choice and self-control, and also with the power, if he wishes, to please God. Now it pleases God that there be no wickedness in man. And if beautiful deeds and the virtues of holy and God-loving souls are praised, while ugly and wicked ones are condemned, how much more are the former dear to God while the latter are condemned?

100. Man receives good things from God, since He is good. It is for this that man was created by God. But man brings evils on himself by himself, by the wickedness within him, by his base desires and his insensibility.

101. The thoughtless soul, although immortal and in principle master of the body, is a slave of the body through pleasures, not perceiving that indulgence

of the body is injurious to the soul. Being insensible and foolish, such a soul takes thought for the indulgence of the body.[63]

102. God is good, man is wicked. There is no evil in Heaven and no abiding goodness on earth. The rational man chooses what is better and knows the God of all, and thanks and praises God in hymns. And before death he feels aversion towards the body, and does not allow evil impulses to be fulfilled, knowing their destructive effect and action.

103. The evil man loves greed and despises justice. He does not reckon the uncertainty, the inconstancy, and the brevity of life, or ponder the fact that death cannot be bribed and is inexorable. And if he is an old man, he is shameless and foolish; he is like rotten wood, of no use for anything.

104. After receiving experience of painful things we can feel pleasures and joy. For one does not drink with pleasure if he is not thirsty, or eat with relish if he is not hungry, or sleep pleasantly if he is not very

[63] Cf. Christ: "Therefore, I say unto you, take no thought for your life, what ye shall eat, or what ye shall drink; nor yet for your body, what ye shall put on. Is not the life more than food, and the body more than raiment?" (*Matthew* 6: 25); and St. Paul: "Put on the Lord Jesus Christ, and make not provision for the flesh, to fulfill the lusts thereof" (*Romans* 13: 14).

sleepy, or feel joy if he has not previously been sorrowful. Likewise, we will not enjoy the eternal goods unless we despise the short-lived ones.

105. Speech is a servant of the mind. For what the mind wishes, this speech interprets.

106. The mind sees all things, including those in the heavens. Nothing darkens it, except sin. To the pure mind nothing is incomprehensible, just as for speech nothing is incapable of being expressed.

107. So far as his body is concerned, man is mortal; but by reason of his mind and speech[64] he is immortal. Being silent, you understand; having understood, you speak. For silence in the mind gives birth to speech. And grateful speech when addressed to God gains man's salvation (σωτηρία).

108. He who says foolish things is mindless. For he speaks without understanding anything. You, however, should consider what is to your interest to do for the salvation of your soul.

109. Speech which is intelligent and profitable to the soul is a gift of God, just as speech that is full of babbling and seeks the dimensions and distances of

[64] There is mental speech and there is physical speech. Regarding mental speech St. Nikephoros the Solitary says: "Within our breast, when our lips are silent, we speak, deliberate, pray, and psalmodize" (Φιλοκαλία, Vol. IV, Athens, 1961, p. 27).

the sky and the earth, and the sizes of the sun and of the stars is an invention of a man who labors in vain. For bragging, he seeks in vain for things that are not at all profitable.

110. No one sees Heaven and is able to know the things in it, except the man who takes care to lead a virtuous life and knows and glorifies God Who created him for salvation and to lead the life of a man. Such a God-loving man knows with certainty that without God nothing exists. God is everywhere and in all things, being infinite.

111. Just as man comes out of the maternal womb, so at death the soul comes out of the body naked. One soul comes out of the body pure and bright; another, with blemishes, its faults; another, black from its many sins. Therefore, the rational and God-loving soul, remembering and considering the evils that follow death, leads a pious life, lest it be condemned to suffer them. Unbelievers, who are foolish in soul, act impiously and sin, not reckoning the things in the other world.

112. Just as when you come out of the womb you do not remember the occurrences in the womb, so when you have come out of the body you do not recall the events when you were in the body.

113. Just as when you came out of the womb you

became stronger and bigger in body, so when you come out of the body pure and unblemished you will be stronger and incorruptible, living in Heaven.

114. Just as the body, when developed in the womb, must be born, so the soul, when it has completed in the body the period of time assigned by God, must come out of the body.

115. When the soul has come out of the body, it will treat you in the same way in which you treated it when it was in the body. He who has pampered his body has treated himself ill for the afterlife. As a fool, he has condemned his soul.

116. Just as the body which comes out of the womb of the mother imperfect cannot be brought up, so the soul which has come out of the body without having acquired knowledge of God through a virtuous way of life cannot be saved or be united with God.

117. The body, united with the soul, comes out of the darkness of the womb into the light. The soul, united with the body, is conjoined with the darkness of the body.[65] Therefore, we must discipline the body.[66] A multitude of foods and dainties excite the passions

[65] Cf. Letter VI of St. Antony; where he speaks of the body as "this house of clay and darkness" (*Letters of St. Antony the Great*, p. 21).

[66] Cf. St. Paul: "Those who belong to Christ Jesus have crucified the flesh with its passions and desires" (*Galatians* 5: 24).

of vice in man, whereas restraint of the belly humbles the passions and is conducive to the salvation
of the soul.

118. The eyes are the organs of sight of the body,
while the mind is the organ of sight of the soul. And
just as a body that has no eyes is blind, and does not
see the sun which illuminates the whole earth and
sea, and is unable to enjoy the light, so the soul which
does not have a good mind and a virtuous way of life
is blind and does not understand God, the Creator
and Benefactor of all the creatures, and does not glorify Him, and cannot enjoy His incorruptibility and
the eternal blessings.

119. Ignorance of God is insensibility and foolishness of soul. For evil arises from ignorance, while
goodness comes to men from knowledge of God
and saves the soul. Therefore, if you endeavor not to
gratify your bad desires, being watchful (νηφάλιος)[67]
and knowing God, you have your mind turned to
the virtues. If, however, you endeavor to fulfill your
bad desires for the sake of pleasure, being drunken
by ignorance of God, you perish like the irrational
animals, not reflecting on the evils that will befall
you after death.

120. The things that happen according to Divine

[67] See also § 54 and the note.

necessity—for example, the daily rising and setting of the sun, and the bearing of fruits by the earth—are part of Divine providence. Similarly, the things that happen according to human necessity are called law. Everything has been made for man.

121. Whatever God does, since He is good, He does for man. Whatever man does, however, he does for himself, both what is good and what is evil. In order that you might not wonder at the happiness of the wicked, realize that just as cities have executioners and do not praise their very evil will, but through them punish those who deserve punishment, in the same manner God allows the wicked to oppress with reference to worldly things, so that through them the impious might be punished. Afterward, He delivers them also to judgment, because they caused suffering to men by not ministering to God but serving their own wickedness.

122. If those who worship idols knew and saw in their heart what they worshipped, they would not have gone astray from piety. Perceiving the beauty, the order, and the providence exhibited by the things made and being made by God, they would have known Him Who created them for man.

123. Man, when bad and unjust, can kill. However, God does not cease granting life to the unworthy.

Being free form envy and good in nature, He willed that the world be made and it was made. And it is made for man and his salvation.

124. A man, in the strict sense, is he who has understood what the body is: that it is corruptible and short-lived. Such an individual also understands what the soul is: that it is divine, immortal, and an in-breathing of God,[68] and was conjoined with the body to be tested and attain theosis (ἀποθέωσις). He who has understood the nature of the soul conducts himself in a manner that is right and pleasing to God. He does not yield to the body, and with his mind he sees God and the eternal goods which are granted to the soul by God.

125. Being ever without envy, God gave to man power over good and evil, having granted to him knowledge, in order that by contemplating the world, and the things in the world, he might come to know Him Who created all things for the sake of man. In the case of the impious man, however, it is possible to desire and not understand. It is possible for him not to believe, to fail, and to think what is contrary to the truth. Such is man's power over good and evil.

[68] Cf. *Genesis*, 2: 7: "And God breathed upon his face the breath of life, and the man became a living soul" (Septuagint).

126. It is an ordinance of God that as the body grows the soul be filled with mind, in order that it may choose out of good and evil that which it likes. A soul which does not choose what is good is devoid of a God-loving mind. Therefore, all human bodies have souls, but not every soul can be said to have such a mind. For a God-loving mind is present in those who are temperate, holy, just, pure, good, merciful, and pious. And the presence of such a mind helps a man in his relation to God.

127. One thing is not possible to man, to be deathless, so far as his body is concerned. To attain union with God (Θεῷ συναφθῆναι) is possible, if one understands how this is possible. For if he wishes, comprehends, believes and loves, through his virtuous life he communes with God (Θεοῦ συνόμιλος γίνεται).

128. The eye beholds visible things. The mind, however, perceives the invisible. For the God-loving mind is light to the soul. He who has a God-loving mind is illumined in his heart and sees God with his mind.

129. No one who is good is ugly in soul; but he who is not beautiful in soul is surely bad and a lover of the body. Now the first virtue of man is contempt of the flesh. For detachment from things transitory, corruptible, material—detachment that is freely chosen and not a result of poverty—renders us heirs of

eternal and incorruptible goods.

130. He who has a mind knows what he is: that he is a mortal man. And he who knows himself knows all things,[69] that they are creatures of God and were made for the salvation of man. For it is in the power of man to understand and believe everything rightly. A man who understands and believes everything rightly knows with certainty that those who despise worldly things toil and trouble themselves least, and receive from God eternal bliss and rest after death.

131. Just as the body is dead without the soul, so the soul, without the intellectual faculty (τὸ νοητικόν) is idle and unable to inherit God.

132. Only to man does God listen. Only to man does God manifest Himself. God loves man, and wherever man may be there also is God. Only man is a worthy worshipper of God. It is for man that God transfigures Himself (μεταμορφοῦται).[70]

133. God created for man the whole firmament and the stars that adorn it. He created for man the

---

[69] Cf. *The Letters of St. Antony*: "Know yourselves" (III, p. 10); "He who knows himself knows God" (III, p. 11); "I write to you as reasonable men, who have been able to know yourselves. For he who knows himself knows God and knows his time" (IV, p. 12).

[70] *Matthew* 17:2: "And Jesus was transfigured before Peter, James, and John."

earth. Men cultivate it for themselves. Those who do not perceive God's providence, which is so great, are foolish in soul.

134. Beauty (τὸ καλόν), such as that of the firmament,[71] is invisible (to those who are unregenerate). Evil is manifest, as are the things on the earth. That is beautiful which is incomparable. The rational man chooses that which is superior in beauty. It is only by man that God and His creatures are apprehended.

135. Mind manifests itself in the soul, and nature manifests itself in the body. Mind is conducive to the theosis of the soul, while the nature of the body is to be subject to decomposition. Nature is present in all human bodies, but (active) mind is not present in every soul. Wherefore, not every human soul is saved.

136. The soul is in the world, since it is begotten (γεννητή). The soul that understands the world and wishes to be saved has at every hour an inviolable law and reflects within itself that the struggle (ἀγών) and test is now, and there is no checking of the judge; and that the soul perishes or is saved through indulging in, or abstaining from, a small shameful pleasure.

137. On earth, birth and death were established by God; in the firmament, providence and necessity.

---

[71] Cf. St. John Climacos: "The firmament has as its beauty the stars" (*The Ladder of Divine Ascent*, Step 29).

And all things were made for man and his salvation. Being free from need of anything, God created the heaven and the earth and the elements for men, through them lavishing upon men every enjoyment of good things.

138. The mortal are subject to the immortal. But the immortal [in the sense of enduring over a long period of time], that is, the elements, serve man through the benevolence and inherent goodness of God Who created them.

139. He who is poor and thereby unable to harm another is not reckoned among the pious in his actions. He, however, who is able to harm another and does not use his power for doing evil, but is merciful to the lowly out of his reverence for God, becomes a recipient of good rewards in this life and after death.

140. Through God's love for man (φιλανθρωπία),[72] there are many paths (όδοί)[73] that lead men to salvation, ways that convert men and lead them to the Heavens. For the souls of men receive rewards for their virtue and punishments for their trespasses.

141. The Son is in the Father, and the Spirit is in the

[72] Cf. *Titus* 3: 4: "The kindness and love (χρηστότης καὶ φιλανθρωπία) of God our Savior towards man."

[73] Cf. *Psalm* 24 (25): 4: "Show me Thy ways, O Lord, and teach me Thy paths." (Septuagint).

Son, and the Father is in both.[74] Through faith man knows all the invisible and intelligible things. Faith is the voluntary assent of the soul.

142. Just as those who for certain needs or by circumstances are forced to swim across the biggest rivers are saved if they are wide-awake (νήφωσι)—for even if the currents happen to be violent and they are submerged for a brief time, by grasping any of the plants that grow on the banks they are saved, whereas those who are drunk, even if they have practiced swimming ten thousand times to perfection, being overcome by wine are covered up by the current and are cut off from the living—in the same way the soul which falls into the distractions of the currents of life, unless it wakes up[75] from the evil of materialism, and realizes its own nature—that it is divine and immortal, and has been joined as a test to the short-lived, subject to many passions, matter of the body—is dragged down to perdition by the

[74] We have here a clear affirmation of the Orthodox doctrine of the Holy Trinity. Cf. St. Athanasios the Great: "Saint Antony taught the people that the Son of God is the eternal Logos and Wisdom of the Essence of the Father" (*Life of Saint Antony*, § 69). Cf. *The Letters of St. Antony the Great*, Letter 2, p. 6: "The Only-begotten is the very Mind of the Father and His image."

[75] Here is emphasized the hesychast practice of inner wakefulness (νῆψις).

pleasures of the body. Despising itself, drunk with ignorance, and not laying hold of itself, the soul perishes and is cut off from the living. For the body often drags us down[76] like a river to unseemly pleasures.

143. The rational soul, abiding unmoved in its good deliberate choice, drives like horses the spirited and appetitive powers of the soul, which are non-rational. And conquering, restraining, and prevailing over them, the soul is crowned and is deemed worthy of life in the Heavens. It receives this prize from God, its Creator, for its victory and toils.

144. The truly rational soul, seeing the happiness of the wicked and the prosperity of the unworthy, is not disturbed by imagining their enjoyment in this life, as do thoughtless men. For it knows clearly both the inconstancy of fortune and the uncertainty and brevity of life, and the fact that Judgment is beyond bribery. Such a soul believes that it is not neglected by God so far as its necessary food is concerned.

145. The carnal life, and the enjoyment of our life here with great wealth and power, is death to the soul. On the other hand, effort, patience, and privation, accompanied by gratitude, and the mortification of the body, is life and eternal pleasure for the soul.

---

[76] Cf. St. Antony's Letter VI, p. 20, where he speaks of "this heavy body."

146. The rational soul, despising the material world and this short life, chooses heavenly bliss and the eternal life, and receives it from God through virtuous living.

147. Those whose clothing is filthy defile the garments of those who rub against them. Similarly, those who are of an evil disposition, and do not lead a right way of life, defile as by filth, through the sense of hearing, the souls of the simple by associating with them and saying improper things.[77]

148. The beginning of sin (ἁμαρτία) is evil desire, through which the rational soul is undermined. On the other hand, salvation (σωτηρία) and the attainment of the Kingdom of Heaven (ἡ Βασιλεία Οὐρανῶν)[78] is love (ἀγάπη) in the soul.[79]

149. Just as copper, when it is not used and does not receive due care rots and becomes useless and devoid of beauty from the verdigris which results from its non-use over a long period of time, so also the soul when it remains idle and does not concern itself with the virtuous way of life and turning to-

---

[77] Cf. St. Paul: "Bad company corrupts good morals" (*I Corinthians* 15: 33).

[78] A very important New Testament expression.

[79] This is consonant with Christ's commandments of love of God and love of neighbor, "on which hang all the law and the prophets" (*Matthew* 23: 37-40).

wards God, and separates itself from the protection
of God through its evil acts, is consumed by the evil
that results in the body from sloth. The soul becomes
devoid of beauty (ἀκαλλής)[80] and incapable of attaining salvation.

150. God is good, passion-free, and unchanging.
Now if one considers it reasonable and true that God
does not change, but is perplexed how He rejoices at
the good, turns away from the wicked, and is angry
at sinners, but gracious when propitiated, it must
be said that God neither rejoices nor is angered. For
to rejoice and to be grieved are passions. Nor is He
propitiated by gifts, for He would be overcome by
pleasure. It is not in the nature of the Deity to be
well or ill disposed by human things. God is good
and only benefits, never harms, always remaining
the same. And we, by remaining good, through likeness (ὁμοιότης) attain union with God; whereas by
becoming evil, through unlikeness (ἀνομοιότης) we
are separated from God.[81] By living virtuously, we
cleave to God, but by becoming wicked we make
God our enemy, not as being angered at us, but in
that our sinful acts do not let God shine within us,

[80] Here we have another expression of the motif that runs
through the *Philokalia*, that of spiritual beauty.
[81] A basic Orthodox teaching.

but join us with malicious demons. If through our prayers and beneficences we find deliverance form our sinful acts, this does not mean that we propitiate and change God, but that through our deeds and our turning to God we cure our wickedness and enjoy again the goodness of God. Hence, it is like saying that God turns away from the wicked and that the sun hides itself from those who lack sight.

151. The pious soul (εὐσεβής ψυχή) knows God, the Creator of all things. For piety (εὐσέβεια) is nothing else but doing the will of God, which is knowledge of God by being free of envy, chaste, meek, agreeable so far as possible, sociable, not fond of strife, and everything else that is pleasing to the will of God.

152. Knowledge of God and fear of Him are a cure of materialistic passions. For when ignorance is present in the soul, the passions remain incurable and the soul decays from wickedness as from a chronic ulcer. God is not the cause of this, for He sent down upon man understanding and knowledge.[82]

153. God filled man with understanding and knowledge, endeavoring to clear away the passions and self-willed wickedness, and wishing through

[82] Cf. Christ: "I will send the Comforter (the Holy Spirit) unto you.... When He, the Spirit of truth, is come, He will guide you into all truth" (*John* 16: 7, 13).

His goodness to change the mortal into immortal.

154. Mind in a pure and God-loving soul truly sees God the unbegotten, unseen, and indescribable, Whose purity is apprehended by those alone who are pure in heart.[83]

155. To bear misfortune in good spirits and gratefully is a crown of incorruptibility, virtue, and salvation of man. And to control anger, the tongue, the belly, and pleasure is an exceedingly great aid to the soul.

156. The power that controls the universe is God's providence. There is no place that is without His providence. This is the self-sufficient Logos[84] of God, Who impresses form on the matter that comes into the world, and is the Creator and Artist ($\Delta\eta\mu\iota\upsilon\varrho\gamma\dot{\varsigma}$ $\kappa\alpha\grave{\iota}$ $\tau\epsilon\chi\nu\dot{\iota}\tau\eta\varsigma$)[85] of all things. For it is not possible for matter to be ordered without the distinguishing power of the Logos, Who is the image ($\epsilon\grave{\iota}\kappa\dot{\omega}\nu$),[86]

[83] Cf. Christ: "Blessed are the pure in heart, for they shall see God" (*Matthew* 5: 8).

[84] Cf. *John*: "In the beginning was the Logos, and the Logos was with God, and the Logos was God." (1:1).

[85] Cf. St. Paul, *Hebrews*, 11: 10: "For he looked for a city which hath foundations, whose Artist and Creator ($\tau\epsilon\chi\nu\dot{\iota}\tau\eta\varsigma$ $\kappa\alpha\grave{\iota}$ $\delta\eta\mu\iota\upsilon\varrho\gamma\dot{\varsigma}$) is God."

[86] Cf. St. Paul, 2 *Corinthians* 4: 4: "Christ Who is the image ($\epsilon\grave{\iota}\kappa\dot{\omega}\nu$) of God."

mind (νοῦς),[87] and wisdom (σοφία),[88] and providence (πρόνοια) of God.

157. Desire that arises from thought is the root of the passions that are akin to darkness. And when the soul lingers on the thought of the desire, it ignores itself, that it is a breath of God.[89] Thus it is borne to sin, being foolish and not reckoning the torments after death.

158. An exceedingly great and incurable disease of the soul and its perdition is godlessness (ἀθεότης) and the love of glory. The desire for evil is a privation of good. Now goodness consists in performing without envy all beautiful deeds that are pleasing to God.

159. Man alone is receptive of God. For to this living creature alone does God speak, at night through dreams,[90] in the daytime through the mind. And through all means He foretells and pre-signifies future goods to those men who are worthy of Him.

160. It is not at all difficult, to him who believes

---

[87] Cf. St. Paul, *1 Corinthians* 2: 16: "But we have the mind (νοῦς) of Christ."

[88] Cf. St. Paul, *1 Corinthians* 1: 24: "Christ is the power of God, and the wisdom (σοφία) of God."

[89] *Genesis* 2: 7.

[90] Cf. St. Gregory of Nyssa: "Some dreams, rare ones, are given to some few who are deemed worthy of evident Divine communication" (*A Select Library of Nicene and Post-Nicene Fathers*, Second Series, ed. by P. Schaff and H. Wace, Vol. V, p. 402).

and wishes, to apprehend God. If you wish to see Him, look at the beautiful order (εὐκοσμία) and providence manifested by all things that have been made and are being made through His Logos.[91] All for man.

161. He is called a saint (ἅγιος) who is pure, free of evil and sin. Wherefore, the absence of evil in man is an exceedingly great attainment of the soul and is pleasing to God.

162. A name is the signification of one entity among many. Wherefore it is foolish to think that God, Who is one and only, has another name. For the name God (Θεός) signifies Him Who is beginningless and has created all things for man.

163. If you are aware that you perform evil acts, cut off such acts from your soul by the expectation of blessings. For God is just and loves man (φιλάνθρωπος).

164. He who endeavors to be always unseparated from God knows God and is known by God. A man becomes unseparated from God by being good with respect to all matters and possessing self-restraint with regard to all pleasures, not because occasions for pleasures do not arise in his life, but because of his firm resolve and self-control.

[91] Cf. text § 156 above.

165. Do good to him who wrongs you,[92] and you shall have God as your friend. Do not slander your enemy to anyone. Exercise love, temperance, patience, self-restraint, and the like. For this is knowledge of God: following God through humility[93] and similar virtues. These are deeds not of chance persons, but of souls with spiritual perception.

166. Because there are some who impiously dare to say that plants and vegetables have soul, I have written this text for the information of the simple. Plants have natural life (ζωή), but they do not have soul (ψυχή). Man is called a rational animal (λογικὸν ζῷον), because he has mind and is capable of acquiring knowledge. The other animals, both those of the land and those of the air have voice (φωνή), because they possess breath and soul. All beings that increase and decrease in size are living, because they live and grow; but not all of them have a soul. There are four kinds of living beings: some have soul and are immortal, such as the Angels (Ἄγγελοι). Others have mind (νοῦς), soul, and breath, such are men. Others have soul and breath, such are the animals (τὰ ζῷα). And

---

[92] Cf. Christ: "I say unto you, Love your enemies, bless them that curse you, do good to them that hate you, and pray for them who despitefully use you and persecute you" (*Matthew* 5: 44).

[93] Cf. St. Paul: "Serving the Lord with all humility of mind" (*Acts* 20: 19).

others have only life (ζωή), such are the plants (τὰ
φυτά). The life of plants is without soul, breath, mind,
and immortality. And all the others (mentioned) cannot be without life. And it is clear that every human
soul is ever in motion from one place to another.[94]

167. When a fantasy of some pleasure arises in
you, guard yourself (φύλασσε σαυτόν)[95] lest you
be carried away by it. Set yourself quickly above it,
remember death and ponder that it is better to be
conscious of yourself (συνειδέναι σεαυτῷ) that you
have overcome the deceit of pleasure.

168. Just as birth is accompanied by passion—for
that which comes into being in life is accompanied
by corruption—so also in passion there is badness.
Do not say that God could not eliminate badness.
Those who say this speak in a state of insensibility
and foolishness. It was not necessary that God make
an end of materiality. For these passions pertain to
materiality. God eliminated badness from men according to what is to their interest. He did this by
bestowing upon them mind, understanding, knowledge, and discrimination between good and evil, so
that knowing badness, that we are harmed by it, we

[94] Of mental space; that is from one object of the mind to
another.

[95] Guarding of oneself, or the soul, is a practice taught and
emphasized throughout the *Philokalia*.

might avoid it. However, the foolish man (ὁ ἀνόητος) follows after badness and is proud of it. And just as if he had fallen into a net, he struggles trapped inside it. And he is never able to look up and see and know God, Who created all things for the salvation and theosis (ἀποθέωσις) of man.

169. Mortal beings are sorry because they know in advance that they will die. Immortality (τὸ ἀθάνατον), being good, comes to the holy soul (ὁσία ψυχή). Mortality (τὸ θνητόν), on the other hand, being evil, comes to the foolish and wretched soul.[96]

170. When happily you betake yourself to your bed, recalling the benefactions and great providence of God, being filled with these good thoughts, you rejoice more. And the sleep of your body becomes wakefulness (νῆψις) to your soul, and the closing of your eyes becomes a true vision (ὅρασις) of God. And your silence, being full of goodness, offers with all your soul and strength extended conscious glory to the God of all.[97] For when badness is absent from man, gratitude alone, more than any sumptuous sacrifice, pleases God. To Him let there be glory unto the ages of ages. Amen.

[96] According to the holy Church Fathers, mortality consists in separation from God and enslavement to sin.

[97] Cf. Christ: "Thou shalt love the Lord thy God with all thy heart and with all thy soul, and with all thy mind, and with all thy strength: this is the first commandment" (*Mark* 12: 30).

CHAPTER 2

BRIEF BIOGRAPHY OF
ST. ISAIAH THE ANCHORITE

Our Holy Father Isaiah the Anchorite flourished around the year 370 A.D. He was a contemporary of Abba Macarios the Great.[1] Having studied the Holy Scriptures night and day, and drawn abundantly spiritual wisdom from these springs of salvation, he became the author of many exceedingly beautiful discourses. These contain various edifying discussions that make up a whole book. From them we picked out and present this brief discourse for those who wish to guard their mind. It teaches in brief compass how one must repel the suggestions of thoughts and have an uncondemning conscience. It also teaches how to meditate and how very calmly and scientifically to guard the three parts of the soul.[2]

---

[1] Also known as Saint Macarios the Egyptian.
[2] The rational part, the spirited, and the appetitive.

SAINT ISAIAH THE ANCHORITE

SAINT ISAIAH THE ANCHORITE

ON GUARDING OF THE MIND

In 27 Texts

1. Anger of the mind (τοῦ νοὸς ὀργὴ) against the passions is according to nature (κατὰ φύσιν). Without such anger purity does not result in man—if the mind does not become angry at all that is sowed in it by the enemy. When Job found the enemy, he (Job) reproached them saying to them: "You who are dishonorable and of no repute, in want of every good thing, whom I did not consider worthy to be with my shepherd dogs!"[3] Now he who wants to acquire anger according to nature cuts off all his volitions, until he establishes himself in the state of the mind that is according to nature.

2. If you are resisting the assault of hatred and see the assault becoming weak and retreating from you, let not your heart rejoice, because the wickedness of the evil spirits has not been exhausted. They are preparing a war worse than the first, and they

[3] Job 30: 4, 1.

left it behind in the city, and command it not to stir.
If you resist, go against them, they flee in weakness
from your presence. And if your heart becomes exalted, because you have driven them away, and you
seize the city, some of them rise from behind, while
others stand in front and let your wretched soul in
their midst, having no longer a place of refuge. Now
the "city" is prayer (εὐχή). Resistance (ἔνστασις) is
the act of contradicting (ἀντιλογία) in the name of
Christ. And the basis is anger according to nature.

3. Let us, therefore, my beloved ones, stand firm
with fear of God, preserving and guarding the practice of the virtues, not offering a stumbling block to
our conscience (συνείδησις), but observing our conscience with fear of God, until it frees itself, so that a
union (ἕνωσις) between us and our conscience takes
place, and our conscience becomes henceforth our
guard (φύλαξ), showing us where we are stumbling.
If we do not obey our conscience, it will retire from
us and abandon us, and we will fall into the hands
of our enemies, and they will no longer leave us. As
our Master has shown us, saying: "Agree with thine
adversary (ἀντίδικος) while thou art in the way with
him," and so on.[4] They say that conscience is "the
adversary," because it opposes the man who wishes

[4] *Matthew* 5: 25.

to do the desire of the flesh. And if a man does not listen to it, conscience surrenders him into the hands of his enemies.

4. If God sees that the mind has submitted to Him with all its power, and has no other help except Him, He strengthens it, saying: "Fear not, my son Jacob."[5] Again, He says: "Fear not: for I have redeemed thee, I have called thee by thy name; thou art mine. And if thou pass through water, I am with thee; and the rivers shall not overflow thee; and if thou go through fire, thou shalt not be burned; the flame shall not burn thee. For I am the Lord thy God, the Holy One of Israel, Who saves thee."[6]

5. If, therefore, the mind hears this boldness, it acts boldly towards the enemy, saying: "Who is it that is fighting against me? Let him stand up against me. Who is that is opposing me? Let him approach me. Behold, the Lord is my helper, who will hurt me? Behold, "all ye shall wax old as a garment by moth."[7]

6. If your heart has by nature hated sin, it has overcome and has withdrawn itself from those who beget sin, and has imparted to you remembrance of

[5] *Isaiah* 41: 13 (Septuagint).
[6] *Ibid.*, 43: 1-3..
[7] *Ibid.*, 50: 8-9.

hell. And know that your Helper abides with you. And you, grieving Him in nothing, but weeping before Him, say: "Thine is the mercy, and redeem me, O Lord. For my hands are without power to escape from the enemy without Thy help." And turn your attention to your heart, and He will safeguard you from every evil.

7. A monk ought to shut all *the gates of his soul, that is, the senses* (αἰσθήσεις),[8] lest through them he be caused to fall. And if the mind sees itself not being gained possession of by anything, he is preparing himself for immortality, gathering his senses together to the same point and making them one body.

8. If your mind is freed from every hope of the world of visible things, this is a sign that sin in you has died.

9. If your mind is freed, the barrier between itself and God departs.

10. If the mind is freed from all its enemies and is at rest, it is in another, new age, thinking new, incorruptible things.

11. Demons restrain themselves for a time, cunningly, hoping that a man will open up his heart, thinking that he has found rest. And suddenly, they jump into the wretched soul and seize it like a spar-

---

[8] Sight, hearing, smell, taste, and touch.

row. And if they gain the upper hand, they humble it mercilessly by means of every sin worse than those for which previously it prayed to be forgiven. Let us, therefore, stand with fear of God and *guard our heart* (φυλάξωμεν τῇ καρδίᾳ), performing the good practices, guarding the virtues, which hinder the wickedness of our enemies.

12. Our teacher Jesus Christ, knowing the great mercilessness of the demons, and having compassion on the race of men, sternly enjoined: "Be ye ready at every hour, for ye know not in what watch the thief will come," lest he come and find you sleeping.[9] Again, He says: "Take heed to yourselves, lest at any time your hearts be overcharged with surfeiting and drunkenness, and cares of this life, and so that day come upon you unawares."[10] Stand, therefore, at the gate of your heart, observing your senses. And if remembrance of God (μνήμη τοῦ Θεοῦ) proceeds in you peaceably, you will catch the thieves trying secretly to take it away. For he who carefully investigates his thoughts (λογισμοί) knows those which are about to enter and defile him. For they agitate the mind, so that it might become distracted and idle. Those, however, who recognize the badness of the

[9] *Matthew* 24: 42-44.
[10] *Luke* 21: 34.

thoughts remain undisturbed, praying to God.

13. Unless a man comes to hate all the works of this world he cannot worship God. What is the nature of worship of God, but this, that we have nothing alien in our mind when we are praying: neither pleasure, when we are praising Him; nor badness, when chanting to Him; nor hatred, in preferring Him before everything else; nor evil zeal hindering us when we are meditating on Him and remembering Him. For all these things are dark; they are a wall surrounding our wretched soul, and it cannot worship God purely, having these things within it. They hinder it in its path and do not allow it to meet God and to praise Him in secret, and pray to Him with sweetness of heart that it be illumined by Him. This is always why the mind (νοῦς) is darkened and cannot advance according to God, because it does not take thought to cut off with knowledge these darkening things.

14. When the mind keeps the senses from desire of the flesh, and leads them to freedom from the passions, and separates the soul from desires of the flesh, then, when God sees the shamelessness of the passions, that they rush at the soul to hold fast the senses in sin, and the mind unceasingly cries aloud in secret to God, He sends His help and at once does

away with them all.

15. I entreat you, so long as you are in the body, do not leave your heart unguarded. For just as a farmer cannot be confident about a certain vegetable of his growing up in his field, for he does not know what will happen to it before it has been shut in his storehouse, so a man cannot leave his heart unguarded as long as he breathes. And since a man does not know what passion will come to him until his last breath, he must not leave his heart unguarded so long as he has breath, but must always cry out to God for His help and mercy.

16. He who does not find help in time of war cannot trust in peace either.

17. When, therefore, one separates oneself from the left, he will know exactly all the sinful acts which he has committed against God. For one does not see his sins if he does not separate himself from them by a separation of bitterness. Those who have reached this point have attained to weeping, entreaty, and feeling shame before God, recalling their evil loves of the passions. Let us, therefore, my brethren, struggle as much as we can, and God will help us according to the abundance of His mercy. And if we have not guarded our heart (οὐκ ἐφυλάξαμεν τὴν καρδίαν ἡμῶν) the way our holy Fathers did, at any rate let

us do all that is in our power to guard (φυλάξαι) our bodies sinless, as God asks, and let us trust that at the time of spiritual famine which befalls us He will have mercy upon us together with His saints.

18. He who has given his heart to seek God with piety, truthfully, cannot have the idea that he has pleased God. For as long as his conscience reproves him about certain things that are contrary to nature he is a stranger to freedom. For as long as there is he who reproves, there is also he who accuses. And as long as there is accusation there is no freedom. Therefore, if when you are praying you see nothing at all accusing you of wickedness, you are free and have entered into God's holy rest, according to His will. If you see that the good fruit has been strengthened and is no longer choked by the weeds of the enemy, and that the enemies have not withdrawn of their own accord, persuaded by their craftiness no longer to wage war against your senses; and if the cloud has overshadowed the tent and the sun has not burned you during the day with its heat, nor the moon during the night;[11] if there has been found in you all the equipment of the tent to set it up and to guard it according to the will of God, then, with the help of God you have been victorious. And then He

[11] Cf. *Psalm* 120: 6 (Septuagint).

will overshadow the tent, for it is His.

So long as there is war, man is under fear and trembles, either to win today or to be defeated tomorrow; either to be defeated tomorrow or to be victorious. The struggle binds tightly the heart. Passionlessness (ἀπάθεια), however, is invincible. For it has received the prize and has become free from cares about the role of the three parts of man, for they have attained peace with one another through God. These three parts are the soul, the body, and the spirit. When these three become one through the action of the Holy Spirit, they can no longer be separated.

Therefore, do not think that you have died to sin, so long as you are constrained by your enemies, either when you are awake or during sleep. For as long as wretched man is in the stadium of struggle, he does not have confidence.

19. If the mind (νοῦς) becomes strong and prepares itself to follow the love which extinguishes the passions of the body and does not let anything that is contrary to nature to oppress the heart, then the mind resists the love which is contrary to nature (παρὰ φύσιν), until it separates that love from the things that are according to nature (κατὰ φύσιν).

20. Examine yourself (ἐρεύνησον ἑαυτόν) daily, my brother, observing your heart before God to see

which of the passions is in it. And cast it out of your heart, lest a grievous judgment come upon you.

21.Observe your heart (πρόσεχε τὴν καρδίαν σου), my brother, and be vigilant with regard to your enemies, for they are cunning in their wickedness. And heed in your heart this statement, that it is impossible for a man to do good acts if he does evil ones. This is why our Savior taught us to be vigilant (γρηγορεῖν) saying: "Strait is the gate, and narrow is the way, that leadeth unto life, and few there be that find it."[12]

22.Observe yourself (πρόσεχε σεαυτῷ) therefore, lest something that leads to perdition removes you from the love of God; and guard your heart. And do not become despondent, saying: How shall I guard it, being a sinful man? For when a man abandons sins and returns to God, his repentance regenerates him and makes him wholly new.

23. Everywhere Divine Scripture, both the Old and the New, speaks of guarding the heart (φυλακὴ τῆς καρδίας). Firstly, the melodist David cries aloud: "O ye sons of men, how long will ye be slow of heart?"[13] Again: "Their heart is vain."[14] Concerning those who

---

[12] *Matthew* 7: 14.
[13] *Psalms* 4: 3 (Septuagint).
[14] *Psalms* 5: 10.

think upon vain things, he says: "For he hath said in his heart, I shall not be moved;"[15] and again: "He hath said in his heart, God hath forgotten;"[16] and many other similar things. A monk ought to understand the aim of Scripture: to whom it speaks when it speaks; and continuously to hold fast the struggle of askesis; and to observe (προσέχειν) the suggestions (τὰς προσβολὰς) of the adversary; and like a pilot (κυβερνήτης) to pass the waves guided by Grace, not being diverted from the path, and exercising attention upon himself alone, but in quiet conversing with God with the mind free from wandering and curiosity.

24. Our time demands from us prayer, just as winds and storms and the surging of the sea require a pilot. For we are susceptible to the suggestion of thoughts, both of virtue and of vice, and the master of thoughts is said to be a pious and God-loving faculty of reason. It is proper for us hesychasts (ἡσυχασταί) to distinguish and separate with understanding and inner wakefulness (νυφόντως) the virtues from the vices; to note which virtue to cultivate when brothers and fathers are present, and which to work at when we are alone; and which is the first, which is the second,

[15] *Psalms* 9: 27.
[16] *Psalms* 9: 32.

and which the third; and which passion is of the soul (πάθος ψυχικόν) and which is of the body (πάθος σωματικόν); and through which virtue pride strikes the mind; from which arises vainglory; from which anger approaches; and from which arises gluttony. We ought to purify our thoughts and purge away "every high thing that exalteth itself against the knowledge of God."[17]

25. The first virtue is freedom from cares (ἀμεριμνία). From freedom from cares arises the desire for God. This desire gives birth to anger that is according to nature, which resists everything that is attempted by the enemy. Then the fear of God finds a dwelling in man; and through this fear love is manifested.

26. It is necessary to overthrow the suggestions (προσβολαί) of evil thoughts from the heart by piously contradicting (ἀντιλογία) them during prayer, lest we be found holding converse with God with our lips, but thinking alien things in our heart. For God does not accept from a hesychast (ἡσυχαστής) a prayer that is turbid and disdainful. Scripture everywhere advises guarding the faculties of the soul. If the will (τὸ θέλημα) of the monk submits to the law of God, his mind (νοῦς) also will govern what is subject to it according to His law—I mean all the movements of the soul, especially anger (θυμός) and

[17] 2 *Corinthians* 10: 5.

desire (ἐπιθυμία), for these are subject to reason.[18] We have cultivated virtue and fulfilled justice; we have turned desire towards God and His will, and anger against the devil and sin. Now what is the thing sought? Inner meditation (ἡ κρυπτὴ μελέτη).

27. If shamelessness is sowed in your heart while you are sitting in your cell, watch; resist badness lest it overcome you. Endeavor to remember God, for He observes you, and the things which you think in your heart are open to Him. Say, therefore, to your soul: If you are afraid of sinners like you, lest they see your sins, how much more must you be afraid of God, Who observes all things? And from this counsel fear of God is manifested in your soul. And if you abide with this fear, you remain unmoved by passions, as is written: "They that trust in the Lord shall be as Mount Sion; he that dwelleth in Jerusalem shall never be moved."[19] And in all the things that you do, have God in mind, for He sees into all your thoughts, and you will never sin. To Him be glory unto the ages. Amen.

[18] Here, as well as the very beginning of this treatise, a very apt use is made of Plato's view of the human soul as having three distinct powers: the rational (νοῦς or λόγος), which is the ruling power of the soul, the spirited (θυμός), and the appetite (ἐπιθυμία), and the spirited power of acting as an ally of the rational power, manifesting itself as anger against bad desires, angrily opposing them. (C.C)

[19] *Psalms* 124: 1 (Septuagint).

CHAPTER 3

BRIEF BIOGRAPHY OF
EVAGRIOS THE MONK

Wise and learned Evagrios flourished around the year 380. He was ordained a Reader by Basil the Great, and a Deacon by Basil's brother Gregory of Nyssa. He was educated in sacred learning by Gregory the Theologian, and served him as Archdeacon at the time when Gregory was Patriarch of Constantinople, according to Nikephoros Kallistos (Book 11, chapter 42). Later, renouncing worldly things, he embraced the monastic life.

Being acute in intellectual perception, and very skillful in giving expression to what he grasped, he left many and varied writings. Among them are the present discourse to hesychasts and chapters concerning the discrimination of passions and thoughts. These have been included in the "Φιλοκαλία" because they present to an eminent degree what is needful and profitable.

121

EVAGRIOS THE MONK

EVAGRIOS THE MONK

MONASTIC SKETCH

TEACHING HOW ONE OUGHT TO LEAD A LIFE OF ASKESIS AND QUIETNESS

In *Jeremiah* it is said: "And thou shalt not take thee a wife in this place, for thus saith the Lord concerning the sons and daughters that are born in this place, ... they shall die of grievous death."[1] This shows that, according to the Apostle, "He that is married careth for the things of the world, how to please his wife," and he is divided, and "she that is married careth for the things of the world," how to please her husband."[2] And it is evident that the statement in the Prophet that "they shall die of grievous death" is said not only concerning the sons and daughters who will come into existence from the married life, but also concerning the sons and daughters that are born in their heart, that is, concerning carnal thoughts and desires, as these too will die of the grievous, sick, and faint spirit of this world, and will not attain the heavenly life. The unmarried, on the other hand, says

[1] *Jeremiah* 16: 1-4 (Septuagint).
[2] *1 Corinthians* 7: 32-34.

123

the Apostle, "careth for the things that belong to the Lord, how he may please the Lord,"[3] and produce the ever-fresh and immortal fruits of the eternal life.

Such is the monk. And thus ought a monk to live, abstaining from a woman, not begetting a son or a daughter in the aforementioned sense. Truly, he must be a soldier of Christ, detached from material things (ἄϋλος) and free from cares, outside every thought and action that is concerned with business, as the Apostle says: "No man that warreth entangleth himself with the affairs of this life; that he may please him who hath chosen him to be a soldier."[4]

Let a monk abide in these things, especially he who has renounced all the matter (ὕλη) of this world and has run off to the beautiful and fair (ὡραῖα καὶ καλά) trophies of quietude. For beautiful and fair is the practice of quietude. Indeed, how beautiful and fair! Its yoke is easy and its burden is light.[5] That life is pleasant, leading it is delightful.

Do you, therefore, my dear reader, wish to undertake the monastic life, such as it is, and to run off to the trophies of quietude? Leave, then, the cares of the world, and the principalities and powers that

[3] *1 Corinthians* 7: 32.
[4] *2 Timothy* 2: 4.
[5] Cf. *Matthew* 11: 30.

pertain to them. That is, become detached from material things, free from passions (ἀπαθής) above every worldly desire, in order that, having become alien to the related circumstances, you might rightly attain quietude. For unless one raises himself above these, one will not be able to achieve this way of life.

Adhere to a simple and easy to be despised fare, not seeking many and tempting foods. And if there should arise in you a thought about expensive foods for the sake of hospitality, abandon this thought. Be not at all persuaded by it, through it there lies in ambush the enemy. He lies in ambush in order to withdraw you from quietude. You have our Lord Jesus Christ censuring in a way the soul, in the figure of Martha, that is zealous about such things. He said: "Why, are you occupied and troubled about many things? One thing is needful,"[6] to hear the Divine Word. And He at once added: "Mary hath chosen the good part, which shall not be taken away from her."[7] You also have the example of the widow at Sarepta, with what things she provided hospitality for the Prophet.[8] Even if you have only bread, even if only salt, even if only water, you can gain through

[6] *Luke* 10: 42.
[7] *Ibid*.
[8] *3 Kings* 17: 9 ff (Septuagint)

these the reward for hospitality. Even if you do not have these, but receive a stranger with a good disposition and say something helpful, you may likewise obtain the reward. For it is said, "a word is above a good gift."[9]

Such are the thoughts you should entertain with regard to charity. Watch, therefore, lest you desire to have wealth for distribution to the poor. For this is a deceit of the evil one, often coming to arouse vainglory, and introducing into the mind a cause of busying oneself with many things. You have the widow cited in the Gospel by our Lord Jesus Christ: through two mites she surpassed the conduct and power of the wealthy. For He says: "They cast into the treasury of their abundance; but she cast all her living."[10]

With regard to clothes, do not desire to have more than are sufficient. Take thought only for those which are necessary for the body. "Cast thy care upon the Lord, and He shall provide for you."[11] For He says that He cares for us.[12] If you need foods or clothes, be not ashamed to receive those that are offered to you by others. To be ashamed to receive them is a kind

---

[9] *Wisdom of Sirach* 18: 17.
[10] *Mark* 12: 43-44.
[11] *Psalms* 54: 23 (Septuagint).
[12] *1 Peter* 5: 7.

of pride. If, on the other hand, you have more than enough of these, give to him who does not have. It is thus that God wishes His children to govern themselves. This is why, writing to the Corinthians, the Apostle said regarding those in want: "Let your abundance be a supply for their want, that their abundance also may be a supply for your want; that there may be equality, as it is written: 'He that hath gathered much had nothing over; and he that hath gathered little had no lack.'"[13]

Having, therefore, what is needful for the present time, take no thought for the future, such as a day, or a week, or months. For when tomorrow comes, it will supply what is needed, if you seek above all the Kingdom of Heaven and the righteousness of God. For the Lord says: "Seek ye first the Kingdom of God and His righteousness; and all these things shall be added unto you."[14]

Do not acquire a servant, lest through him the enemy give rise to some scandal and disquiet your mind, making you take thought about very luxurious foods. For you will no longer be able to take thought only for yourself alone. Even if there should

[13] *2 Corinthians* 8: 14-15; *Exodus* 16: 18.
[14] *Matthew* 6: 33.

come the thought of doing this for the sake of bodily rest, think of what is better: I mean spiritual rest. For spiritual rest is truly better than bodily rest. Even if the thought should enter your mind of doing this for the benefit of your servant, be not persuaded. For this is not your work. It is the work of others, of the holy Fathers who live in coenobia. Take thought only for what is of benefit to you, and lead the life of quietude.

Do not desire to dwell with men who are materialistically minded and distracted. Live either alone, or with brothers who are detached from material things and are of one mind as you. For he who dwells with men who are materialistically minded and involved in worldly affairs will no doubt have a share of their distractions and will be subject to human injunctions, to vain talk, and to all the other afflictions: anger, sorrow, mania for material things (τῶν ὑλῶν).

Also, be not carried away by cares for your parents and friendships with relatives. And give up continual social contacts with them, lest these rob you of the quietude of your cell and lead you about their own circumstances. "Let the dead bury their dead," says the Lord, "but come, follow me."[15]

If the cell where you dwell is easily accessible, flee

[15] *Matthew* 8: 22.

from it. Do not have consideration for it and do not give away to fondness of it. Do everything, perform everything in order that you may be able to attain quietude, to have leisure, to strive to abide by the will of God, and to engage in battle against the invisible enemies. If you cannot easily attain quietude in your regions, resolve to go to a foreign land, and urge your thoughts towards this. Be like an excellent trader, proving all things with a view of quietude, and always holding fast to that which is quiet and useful for this.

Moreover, I tell you, love dwelling in a foreign land. It frees you from the circumstances of your own land and makes you enjoy only the benefits of quietude. Avoid tarrying in a city, and persevere dwelling in the wilderness. "Behold," says holy David, "I went far away, and settled in the desert."[16] If possible, do not go to a city at all. For you will see nothing serviceable, nothing useful, nothing profitable for your way of life. The same holy man again remarks: "In the city I saw lawlessness and controversies."[17]

Therefore, seek places that are free from distractions and solitary. Be not afraid of their sounds. Even if you should see there fantasies of the demons, be

[16] *Psalms* 54: 7 (Septuagint).
[17] *Psalms* 54: 9 (Septuagint).

not frightened, and do not flee from the stadium which is beneficial for you. Abide fearlessly, and you will see the magnificent things of God, His help, His care, and every assurance regarding salvation. "I waited patiently," says the blessed man, "for Him Who would save me from loss of courage and from storm."[18] Let not the desire for musing overcome your resolution. For "the wandering of desire perverts the guileless mind."[19] Many temptations result by reason of this. Fear stumbling, and you will be steadfast in your cell.

If you have friends, avoid continual association with them. For if you meet them after long periods of time you will be profitable to them. If you perceive that harm results to you through them, you will not approach them at all. You ought to have friends who are of benefit to you and contribute to your way of life. But avoid association with wicked and quarrelsome men, and do not dwell together with them. Keep away from their evil purposes. They are far from God.

Let peaceful men, spiritual brothers, holy fathers be your friends. The Lord thus calls them. He says: "They are my mother and brethren and father who

[18] *Psalms* 54: 9 (Septuagint).
[19] *Wisdom of Solomon* 4: 12.

do the will of my Father Who is in Heaven."[20]

Do not have dealings with busybodies, and do not attend a banquet with them, lest they draw you to their deceits and lead you away from the science of quietude. For there is this passion in them. Do not turn your ear to their words and do not accept the thoughts of their hearts, because they are harmful. Let the compassion and longing of your heart be for the faithful of the earth, sympathizing with their sorrow. "My eyes are turned towards the faithful of the earth, that they may dwell with me."[21] And if someone of those who live in accordance with the love of God invite you to dinner, and you wish to go, do go, but return quickly to your cell.

If possible, never sleep outside your cell, in order that the gift of quietude might remain continually with you, and your spiritual work will proceed unhindered.

Be not desirous of fine foods. For as the Apostle says, "She that liveth in pleasure is dead while she liveth."[22] Do not fill your belly with alien foods, lest you acquire a longing for them and they create in you the desire for the dining tables of others. For

[20] *Matthew* 12: 49-50.
[21] *Psalms* 101: 6 (Septuagint).
[22] *1 Timothy* 5: 6.

it is said: "Be not deceived by the feeding of the belly."[23] And if you see yourself being continually invited outside your cell, decline the invitation, for the continual sojourn outside your cell is harmful. It deprives of Grace, darkens the mind-set, withers aspiration. Behold an earthen vessel of wine, after being in a place for a long time and lying unmoved, it renders the wine bright, settled, and fragrant. But if it is carried about here and there, the wine becomes turbid, dull, exhibiting all the badness of the dregs. Compare yourself with the wine and derive benefit from this example. Break relations (σχέσεις) with the many, lest your mind become dependent on circumstances that disturb the way of quietude.

Take thought for manual work, if possible both during the day and at night, in order that you might not become a burden to anyone, and indeed might give to others, as Paul the Apostle advises.[24] In this way also you will overthrow the demon of despondency and will banish all the desires of the enemy; for the demon of despondency impends over idleness. And as they say, "Whoever is idle is surrounded by desires."[25]

In giving and receiving you will not escape sin.

[23] *Proverbs* 24: 15 (Septuagint).
[24] 1 *Thessalonians* 2: 9; *Ephesians* 4: 28
[25] *Proverbs* 13: 4 (Septuagint).

Therefore, whether you sell or buy, you cause to yourself a little loss from equality in the exchange. Be not led to the ways of love of profit manifested in strictness about the price, and thus succumb to the things that cause harm to the soul, that is, contentiousness, false oaths, change of your statements, and the like, and thus dishonor your purpose and put your reputation to shame. Therefore, be on your guard in your transactions. And if you choose the better course, and this is possible for you, entrust the care to someone else who is a faithful man, so that thus having become cheerful you might have good and agreeable hopes. These are the useful pieces of advice which the way of quietude is able to give you.

Now bear in mind also the following things which it brings. I shall set them forth and you listen and do what I enjoin. Sitting in your cell, gather your mind together, remember the day of death. Behold then the state of death of the body, reflect on the misfortune, experience the pain, observe the vanity in this world, as well as leniency and zeal, in order that you might be able to abide always by the same purpose of quietude and not weaken.

Remember also the state in hell at this moment. How are the souls there? In what extreme bitter silence? Or in what exceedingly terrible sighs? In what great fear or agony? In what expectations? Remember the unceasing pain, the endless weeping of the soul. Also remember the day of the Resurrection and the standing before God. Imagine that fearful and dreadful Judgment-Seat. Bring to mind what is laid up for those who sin: shame before God and His Christ, before angels, archangels, powers, and all men; and also the means of punishment: the eternal fire, the worm that does not die,[26] Tartaros, the darkness, and in addition to these the gnashing of teeth,[27] and the fear of torments.

Then bring before you the blessings which are laid up for the righteous: confidence with God the Father and His Christ, with angels, archangels, powers and all the people; the Kingdom and its gifts; the gladness and enjoyment.

Bring to yourself the memory of each of these, and sigh and weep over the Judgment of the sinners. Invest the idea with mourning, fearing lest you, too, might be among them. But rejoice exceedingly over the blessings laid up for the righteous, and labor to enjoy the latter and to be delivered from the former. See to it that you never lose thought of these things, whether you happen to be inside your cell or

[26] *Mark* 9: 46.
[27] *Matthew* 8: 12.

somewhere outside it. Do not turn your mind away from memory of them, so that at any rate through these you might abide free from impure and harmful thoughts.

Let your fasting (νηστεία) be according to your power before the Lord; for it purges off your iniquities and sins,[28] exalts the soul, sanctifies the mind, drives away the demons, and prepares one to be near God. Having eaten once a day, do not desire to eat a second time, lest you become extravagant and disquiet your mind. By limiting your meals to one a day, you will be able to do beneficent works and to mortify the passions of your body. However, if there happens to be a meeting of brethren, and it is necessary to have a second and a third meal, be not gloomy and downcast; rather rejoice, becoming obedient to the need. And having eaten a second or even a third time, thank God that you have fulfilled the law of love and that you will have God Himself as the governor of your life. Also, there are occasions when there is bodily sickness and it is necessary to eat a second and a third time or many times. So let not your mind be grieved. One must not be completely inflexible in the ascetic way during sicknesses, but must yield to some extent, in order that he might be disciplined in

[28] *Isaiah* 6: 7.

the efforts that are peculiar to the way.

As far as abstinence from foods (ἀποχὴ βρωμάτων) is concerned, the Divine Logos did not forbid us to eat certain things, but said: "Behold, even as the green herbs have I given you all things,"[29] "eat asking no question;"[30] and "not that which goeth into the mouth defileth a man."[31] Therefore, to abstain from food should be of our own choice and decision.

Bear gladly vigils (ἀγρυπνίαι), sleeping on the ground (χαμευνίαι) and all the other hardships, having regard to the glory that will be revealed to you and to all the saints. "For the sufferings of this present time," says the Apostle, are not worthy to be compared with the glory which shall be revealed in us."[32]

If you are depressed, pray, as it is written.[33] Pray with fear, with trembling, with effort, in a state of inner wakefulness and watchfulness (νηφαλίως και ἐγρηγόρως). You ought to pray in this manner especially because of the mischievous enemies. For whenever they see us standing at prayer, then above all they too stand by us with eagerness, suggesting

[29] *Genesis* 9: 3.
[30] *1 Corinthians* 10: 25.
[31] *Matthew* 15: 11.
[32] *Romans* 8: 18.
[33] Cf. *James* 5: 13.

(ὑποβάλλοντες) to our mind those things which we ought not to recall or think about during prayer. They do this in order to lead our mind away captivated, and render the entreaty and supplication of our prayer vain and useless. For prayer and entreaty and supplication are really vain and useless when, as we said, they are not performed with fear and trembling, and in a state of inner wakefulness and vigilance. When someone approaches a man who is a king, one entreats him with fear, trembling, and attention (νῆψις), ought not one to stand much more in a similar manner before God, the Master of all, and Christ the King of Kings and the Ruler of Rulers, and perform the supplication and entreaty in a like manner? Very much so. For to Him the whole spiritual host, the chorus of Angels, serving with fear and glorifying with trembling, offer up unceasing hymns, and to His Beginningless Father, and to the All-Holy and Coeternal Spirit, now and forever unto the ages of ages. Amen.

BY THE SAME EVAGRIOS
TEXTS
ON DISCRIMINATION OF PASSIONS
AND THOUGHTS

1. Of the demons, who are our adversaries in our spiritual striving, the first that band together in the warfare are those who are entrusted with the appetites of gluttony, those who suggest (ὑποβάλλοντες) the love of money, and those who call us forth to the glory of men. All the others, proceeding after these, receive in succession those who have been wounded by them. For it is not possible to fall into the hands of the spirit of fornication, unless one has fallen as a result of gluttony. And it is not possible to arouse anger in one who is not fighting for food, or money, or glory. And it is not possible to escape the demon of sorrow, if one has suffered privation of all of these things. Nor will one escape pride, the first offspring of the devil, unless one has banished the love of money, the root of all evil, since poverty humbles a man, according to Solomon.[34] And in short, it is not possible for a man to be caused to fall, if he has not been wounded by those front-rank demons.

[34] *Proverbs* 10: 4 (Septuagint).

This is why the devil brought forth the following three thoughts to the Savior: First, he asked that the stones be made bread. Second, he offered the world, if the Savior would fall down and worship him. Third, he said that if He would hearken, He would be glorified and suffer nothing from such a great fall. Our Lord, having shown Himself superior, commanded the devil to get hence,[35] thereby teaching that it is not possible to drive away the devil, unless one has disdain for these three thoughts: gluttony, love of money, and love of human glory.

2. All devilish thoughts bring to the soul ideas of things that are perceived by the bodily senses. Having received these sense-impressions, the mind bears within itself the forms of these objects. Hence, from the object itself that is presented the mind knows which demon is approaching. For example, if the face of the person who has caused me a loss or has dishonored me appears in my mind, the approaching thought of rancor is exposed. Again, if there is a suggestion (ὑπόμνησις) of money, or of glory, clearly the one who is afflicting us will be recognized from the objects suggested. And in the case of other thoughts you will similarly discover,

[35] *Matthew* 4: 1-10.

from the thing suggested, the one who stands by and makes the suggestions. I do not say that all the memories of such things result from demons, because by nature the mind itself, by its own activity, brings up fantasies of things that have happened. I mean only those memories which bring on anger or desire that are contrary to nature. For through the agitation of such anger and desire the mind commits adultery and quarrels, being unable to accept the thought which God legislated to it, although that brightness appears to the ruling faculty (τὸ ἡγεμονικόν) during prayer, when it is deprived of thoughts connected with the senses.

3. Man cannot drive away passionate memories, unless he pays attention to desire and anger, consuming desire through fasts and vigils, and sleeping on the ground, and taming anger through longsuffering, forbearance, forgiveness, and almsgiving. For from these two passions there arise almost all the devilish thoughts which lead the mind to disaster and perdition. It is impossible to overcome these two passions, unless we completely slight foods, possessions, and glory, and even our very body, not being upset by those who often attempt to strike it. There is every need, then, to imitate those who are in danger at sea and throw things overboard on account of the force

of the winds and the rising waves. However, here we must be very careful, lest we cast overboard things in order that we be seen by men (and be praised by them). For then we lose our reward. And we shall suffer another shipwreck, worse than the earlier one, that which results from the contrary wind of the demon of vainglory. For this reason in the Gospels, the Lord, instructing our ruling faculty, the mind, says: "Take heed that ye do not your alms before men, to be seen by them: otherwise ye have no reward of your Father Who is in the Heavens."[36] Again: "When thou prayest, thou shall not be as the hypocrites are: for they love to pray in the synagogues and in the corners of the streets, that they may be seen by men. Verily I say unto you, they have their reward.... And when ye fast, be not as the hypocrites, of a sad countenance: for they disfigure their faces, that they may appear unto men to fast. Verily I say unto you, they have their reward."[37] Watch here the physician of souls, how He cures anger by means of almsgiving; how through prayer He purifies the mind; and how through fasting He causes desire to wither. Through these the New Adam is formed, he who is renewed in the image of his Creator, and in whom, by reason

[36] *Matthew* 6: 1.
[37] *Matthew* 6: 5, 16.

of freedom from passions, there is neither male nor female; and by reason of the one Faith there is "neither Greek nor Jew, circumcision nor uncircumcision, Barbarian nor Scythian, bond nor free, but Christ is all in all."[38]

CONCERNING DREAMS

4. We should enquire how, in the fantasies (φαντασίαι) that occur during sleep, the demons impress on our ruling faculty (τὸ ἡγεμονικόν) and endure it with form; for such a thing seems to happen to the mind, either through the eyes while the mind is seeing, or through the ears while it is hearing, or through any other sense whatsoever; or through the memory, which impresses on the ruling faculty those things which it received through the body, stirring these up. The demons seem to me to impress the ruling faculty by acting on the memory (μνήμη). For the sense-organs are inactive during sleep. So we must ask how the demons activate the memory; whether it is perhaps through the passions. That it is through them is evident from the fact that those who are pure and passionless no longer suffer such a

[38] *Colossians* 3: 10-11.

thing. There is also an activity of the memory which is simple, caused by us or by the holy (angelic) powers, during which activity we meet with saints and feast together with them. However, one must notice that the very images which the soul receives in association with the body, these memories stir without the body. This is clear from the fact that often we experience the same also during sleep, when the body is at rest. For just as it is possible to remember water both while thirsty and while not thirsty, so it is possible to remember gold with greed and without greed. The same is true of other things. However, to find such and such differences between fantasies is a mark of the evil art of demons. At the same time, one must know this, too, that the demons also use external things for producing fantasies, such as the sound of waves in the case of those who are traveling by water.

5. Our anger (θυμός) contributes very much to the aim of demons when it is active in a way that is contrary to nature, and it becomes most useful for all their evil arts. Therefore none of them ceases exciting it both at night and in daytime. But when they see it bound by meekness, they unloose it by means of plausible pretexts, so that having become exceedingly sharp it might serve their ferocious thoughts. Therefore, it is necessary to avoid exciting anger,

whether for just or unjust ends. We must not give an evil sword to those who suggest it. I know many who often do this, being inflamed with anger over small matters. For tell me, for the sake of what do you engage in battle so quickly, if indeed you have come to despise foods, possessions, and glory? And why do you feed the dog (of anger), when you declare that you possess nothing? And if the dog barks and attacks men, it is evident that it possesses some things and wants to guard them. But I believe that such a person is far from pure prayer, because I know that anger banishes such prayer. In addition, I wonder that he forgets the saints. Thus, David cries aloud: "Cease from anger, and forsake wrath."[39] And Ecclesiastes enjoins: "Remove anger from thy heart, and put away evil from thy flesh;"[40] while the Apostle commands that men "lift up holy hands, without wrath and doubting."[41] And are we not taught by the mystic and ancient custom of men of driving dogs out of the house at the time of prayer? This custom teaches in a symbolic way that there should be no anger in those who pray. It is written: "Their wine is the rage of serpents"[42] and the Nazarenes abstained from wine.

[39] *Psalms* 36: 8 (Septuagint).
[40] *Ecclesiastes* 11: 10 (Septuagint).
[41] *1 Timothy* 2: 8.
[42] *Deuteronomy* 32: 33 (Septuagint).

That one ought not to be anxious about clothes and
food is, I think, superfluous to write, inasmuch as the
Savior Himself forbids this in the Gospels. He says:
"Take no thought for your life, what ye shall eat, or
what ye shall drink; nor yet for your body, what ye
shall put on."[43] For this is downright a characteristic of the gentiles and unbelievers, who violate the
providence of the Lord and deny the Creator. Such
a thing is altogether alien for Christians, once they
have believed that two sparrows that are sold for a
farthing[44] are under the governance of the holy angels. This, too, is a practice of the demons: after impure thoughts to introduce thoughts of care, in order
that Jesus might withdraw, owing to the multitude
of thoughts gathered in the place of the mind,[45] and
His teaching might remain without fruit, choked by
thoughts of (worldly) care. Putting these aside, therefore, let us cast our care upon the Lord, being content
with things that we already have, and leading a life
of poverty, wearing shabby clothes, stripping ourselves daily of the causes of vainglory. If someone
thinks that he disgraces himself by wearing shabby

[43] *Matthew* 6: 25.
[44] *Matthew* 10: 29.
[45] Cf. *John* 5: 13.
[46] *2 Timothy* 4: 8; *2 Corinthians* 11:27.

clothes, let him note Saint Paul, who looked for the crown of righteousness "in cold and nakedness."[46] However, since the Apostle called this world a spectacle and a race,[47] let us see whether it is possible for one who has put on cares to run for "the prize of the high calling of God;"[48] or to "wrestle against principalities, against powers, against the rulers of the darkness of this world."[49] I do not see that this is possible, taught even by the history that pertains to the visible world. For it is evident that the runner will be hindered and dragged about by his coat, just as the mind is by cares, if the saying is true that "where your treasure is, there will your heart be also."[50]

6. Of thoughts (λογισμοί), some cut and others are cut. The evil cut the good. Again, evil thoughts are cut by the good ones. The Holy Spirit watches the first thought and condemns us or approves us with reference to it. What I mean is something like this: I have a certain thought of hospitality for the Lord; but when the tempter comes, this thought is cut by the suggestion of offering hospitality for the sake of glory. Again, I have the thought of hospitality in or-

[47] *1 Corinthians* 9: 24.
[48] *Philippians* 3: 14.
[49] *Ephesians* 6: 12.
[50] *Matthew* 6: 21.

der to show off to men. But this, too, is cut when a better thought comes: a thought of directing our virtue of hospitality to the Lord, and not compelling us to offer hospitality for the sake of men.

7. After much observation we have come to know that there is this difference between angelic thoughts (ἀγγελικοὶ λογισμοί), human thoughts (ἀνθρώπινοι λογισμοί), and thoughts that come from demons. Firstly, angelic thoughts enquire about the nature of things and track out their spiritual meaning. For example: for the sake of what was gold made and is scatted like sand in the lower regions of the earth, and is found with much toil and effort? And how, having been found, it is washed in water and committed to the fire, and then is put into the hands of artists who make the candlestand of the tabernacle, the large and the small censers, and the cups,[51] from which, through the Grace of our Savior, the Babylonian king no longer drinks.[52] The heart of Cleopas burns within him by these mysteries.[53]

Demonic thought neither knows nor understands these things. It only shamelessly suggests the acquisition of gold as an object of sight and foretells

[51] See *Exodus* 25: 22-39.
[52] *Daniel* 5: 2, 3.
[53] *Luke* 24: 32.

the food and glory that will come from it. Human thought, on the other hand, neither seeks the acquisition of gold, nor enquires what gold is a symbol of, but only brings to the intellect the bare form of gold, separated from passion and greed. The same account will be given of other objects, too, if it is made to conform inwardly to this canon.

8. There is a demon, called the deceiver (ὁ πλάνος), who comes to brethren at dawn, and leads the mind about from city to city, from village to village, and from home to home, pretending that the visits are innocent. And meeting with some acquaintances for a longer period of time, and spoiling the state that is proper in relation to those one meets, the mind gradually distances itself from the knowledge of God and of virtue, and forgets its vocation. Therefore he who has withdrawn from the world must watch this demon, both whence he comes and where he ends up. For he does not make that long circuit without a purpose and at random. He does this wishing to corrupt the mental state of the anchorite; in order that the mind, having been kindled by these things and become intoxicated by the many visits, might straightway fall to the demon of fornication, or to that of wrath, or to that of sorrow, whereby demons especially destroy the brightness of the state of the mind.

Now if indeed we aim to know clearly the cunning of the demon called the deceiver, let us not be quick to speak to him, or reveal to him that we know his aims, how he is mentally effecting these visits, how he is gradually driving the mind to its death, because he will flee from us. For he does not deign to be seen doing this. And we shall then not perceive any of the things which we wanted to learn. Instead, we should allow him another day, or even a third one, to complete the drama, in order that we might learn his fraud with exactness, and after this examining him by reason we might banish him. However, since during temptation the mind is clouded and does not see with exactitude what is happening, let this be done when the demon has withdrawn. Having sat down, recall in solitude the things that have happened: whence you began, where you went, and at what place you were seized by the spirit of fornication, or of sorrow, or of wrath; and again how the events happened. Examine these things very carefully and commit them to memory, in order that you might have them ready to censure the demon when he approaches you. And make known the place hidden by him, and henceforth you will not follow him. And if you wish to excite him to rage, censure him at once when he comes, and reveal by word the first place which you entered, and the second, and the third. For he becomes very angry, not bearing the disgrace. Let this be a proof that you spoke to him properly, that the thought departed from you. For it is impossible for him to abide when manifestly exposed.

When this demon has been defeated, there follows very heavy sleep and deadness, with much coldness of the eyelids, countless yawnings, and heaviness of shoulders. Through intense prayer all these are dispersed by the Holy Spirit.

9. Hatred against the demons contributes exceedingly to our salvation and is useful for cultivating virtue. However, we do not have the power to bring it up like a good offspring, by ourselves, because the pleasure-loving spirits bear through it and summon forth the soul to friendliness and habit. But this friendliness, or rather this difficult to cure gangrene, is cured by the Physician of souls through abandonment. For He permits us to suffer from them something fearful by night and by day. The soul then returns to the archetypal hatred, being taught to say to the Lord, like David: "I hated them with perfect hatred: they were counted mine enemies."[54] For that individual hates his enemies with perfect hatred who

[54] *Psalms* 138: 22 (Septuagint).

sins neither overtly nor mentally — which is a sign of the greatest and first grade passionlessness.

10. Now what must I say about the demon that renders the soul insensible (ἀναίσθητον)? For I fear to write about him. How the soul departs from its own proper state at the time of his coming and strips itself of fear of God and of devoutness; and does not reckon sin as sin; and does not consider transgression as transgression; and remembers both eternal hell and Judgment as bare words; and indeed laughs at fire-bearing earthquakes; and while in appearance confessing God it does not think of His commandments. When your soul is incited to sin, you beat your breast, but it does not listen. You speak about the Scriptures, but it is wholly insensible and does not hear. You convey to it the shame before men and it does not take that into account, after the manner of a pig that has closed its eyes and broken through the fence.

This demon is brought to the soul by continued thoughts of vainglory. If his days are not shortened, "there should no flesh be saved."[55] For he is among those demons that seldom come to the brethren. The reason is evident: he is banished when some are in a state of misfortune, and others are pressed by dis-

[55] *Matthew* 24: 22.

eases, or are suffering hardships in prison, or meet sudden death. For when the soul experiences little by little contrition and sympathy, the hardness caused by the demon is dissolved. We do not have these things, because of the wilderness where we live and the rareness of sick persons among us. Wanting to banish this demon, the Lord enjoined in the Gospels that we see the sick and visit those in prison. Thus, He says: "I was sick, and ye visited me."[56]

However, one must know this: if some anchorite fell in with this demon and did not receive thoughts of fornication, and did not leave his dwelling-place because of despondency, such a person received patience and chastity descended from the Heavens, and is blessed with such passionlessness. Let those, on the other hand, who profess to practice piety (θε-οσέβειαν),[57] but choose to associate with those in the world, be on their guard against this demon. I myself feel shame before men to say or write more about him.

ON THE DEMON OF SORROW

11. All the demons but one teach the soul to love

[56] *Matthew* 25: 36.
[57] Cf. *1 Timothy* 2: 10.

pleasure; only the demon of sorrow does not deign to do this, but corrupts the thoughts of those into whom he enters. He cuts off and dries up every pleasure of the soul, for "the bones of a sorrowful man dry up."[58] Now if he wages war moderately, he renders the anchorite (ἀναχωρητής) successful. For he persuades him to attach himself to nothing of this world and to shun all pleasures. When, however, he persists obstinately, he begets thoughts that advise the anchorite to give up the spiritual struggle or compel him to flee far away from the place where he is. It is thought that this is what happened to holy Job when he was annoyed by this demon. For he said: "O that I might lay hands upon myself, or at least ask another, and he should do this for me."[59]

The symbol of this demon is the viper, the poisonous beast, whose nature, given with a view to the good of man, destroys the poison of other beasts, but when received in excess destroys the animal itself. It was to this demon that Paul turned over the man who had acted sinfully. Wherefore he writes to the Corinthians telling them to confirm their love towards him, "lest perhaps such a one should be swallowed up with overmuch sorrow."[60] He knew that

[58] *Proverbs* 17: 22.
[59] *Job* 30: 24 (Septuagint).
[60] *2 Corinthians* 2: 7.

this spirit, which affects men, also occasions good repentance. For this reason Saint John the Baptist called those who were goaded by this spirit and sought refuge in God, offsprings of vipers, saying: "Who hath warned you to flee from the wrath to come? Bring forth therefore fruits meet for repentance. And think not to say within yourselves, We have Abraham to our father."[61] However, whosoever has imitated Abraham and has gone forth out of his land out of his kindred,[62] such a one has become stronger than this demon.

12. If one has conquered anger, he has conquered demons. But if one is enslaved to anger, he is alien to the monastic life, and alien to the ways of the Savior, for the Lord Himself is said to teach His ways to the meek.[63] Wherefore, the mind of those who withdraw from the world in order to conquer, have a recourse to the plain of meekness. The great Moses had this virtue: he has been called "very meek, beyond all the men."[64] And holy David declared that meekness is worthy of God's memory, saying: "Lord remember David and all his meekness."[65] Also, the Savior

[61] *Matthew* 3: 7-9.
[62] *Genesis* 12: 1.
[63] *Psalms* 24: 9 (Septuagint).
[64] *Numbers* 12: 3.
[65] *Psalms* 131: 1 (Septuagint).

Himself enjoined us to become imitators of His meekness, saying: "Learn of me; for I am meek and lowly
in heart: and ye shall find rest unto your souls."[66]
Now if one should abstain from food and drinks, but
should excite anger through evil thoughts, he would
be a ship sailing in the open sea and having a demon
as pilot. Therefore, we must pay attention as much
as we can to our dog, that is, anger, and must teach
him to destroy only the wolves and not to eat up the
sheep, exhibiting great meekness towards all human
beings.

ON VAINGLORY

13. Of all the thoughts, only that of vainglory
abounds in materials, encompassing almost the
whole inhabited world and secretly opening the
doors to all the other demons, becoming like a sort
of wicked traitor of a certain city. It exceedingly de-
grades the mind of the individual that has withdrawn
from the world. It fills the mind with many words
and things, and destroys prayer, through which the
mind endeavors to heal all the wounds of the soul.
All the defeated demons join in effecting the growth

---

[66] *Matthew* 11: 29.

of this thought, and through it they enter again into the souls, thus making their last state worse than the first.[67] From this thought springs that of pride, which cast down from Heaven to the earth him who had the seal of likeness (to God) and the crown of beauty. Therefore, we must turn away from that thought, must not linger with it, lest we surrender our life to others and our substance to those who are merciless.[68] This demon is driven away by extended prayer, and by neither doing nor saying anything that contributes to accursed vainglory.

14. When the mind of those who have withdrawn from the world attains a little freedom from the passions, upon acquiring the horse of vainglory runs with it to cities, animated by the great praise of repute. Then, by Divine dispensation, having been assaulted by the spirit of fornication and having been shut up in one of the hog-sties, instructs it not to leave the bed until it has recovered perfect health, and not to imitate the disorderly sick, while still bearing in themselves remnants of their disease unseasonably devote themselves to walks and baths, and thereby relapse into their sickness.

Therefore, sitting down (at our cell) let us exercise

[67] *Matthew* 12: 45.
[68] Cf. *Proverbs* 5: 9.

inner attention, so that as we advance in virtue we may become hard to move towards vice. And awakening in knowledge we may gain many and varied objects of contemplation. And rising higher, we may behold more manifestly the light of our Savior.

15. I cannot write about all the villainies of the demons. And I am ashamed to speak about them at length and in order, fearing that this might have adverse effects on the minds of my readers. However, listen about the cunning of the spirit of fornication. When one has acquired passionlessness (ἀπάθεια) with regard to the appetitive part of the soul (τὸ ἐπιθυμητικὸν μέρος), and shameful thoughts have become somewhat cold, this demon presents men and women playing with one another. He makes the anchorite a spectator of shameful things and gestures. But this temptation is not among those which continue for long. For intense prayer and a very meager fare, together with vigils and the practice of dwelling on spiritual objects of contemplation banish this demon like a waterless cloud. There are times when he even touches the flesh, forcing it to irrational excitement. This cunning demon contrives myriads of other things, which it is not necessary to commit to writing and make public.

Strong anger against this demon greatly helps

one oppose such thoughts. He fears such anger very much when it is directed against thoughts and destroys his designs. This is the meaning of the statement: "Be ye angry and sin not."[69] This anger is a useful medicine to the soul at times of temptation.

The demon of anger imitates this demon, and he, too, forms (in one's mind) images of one's parents, friends, or relatives as being insulted by unworthy persons. And he excites the anger of the anchorite to make him say or do something evil to those abusers who appear to him mentally. It is necessary to exercise attention towards these phenomena and quickly to free the intellect from them, lest, having lingered with them it might become a firebrand during prayer. Those individuals especially fall into these temptations who are irascible and easily enflamed to sensual desires. They are far from prayer and from the knowledge of our Savior Jesus Christ.

16. The Lord handed over the ideas (νοήματα) of this age to man, like sheep, to a good shepherd; and it is written: "He has put the thought into the heart of every man,[70] having conjoined in him desire and anger as aids; in order that through anger he

[69] *Psalms* 4: 5.
[70] Cf. *Hebrews* 10: 16.

might drive away the thoughts of the 'wolves,' while through desire he might feel affection for the 'sheep,' even when often he is exposed to rains and winds. In addition, the Lord has given Law, that he tend the sheep, and a place of green grass and water of rest:"[71] A psalter and a cithara, a rod and a staff; in order that he be fed and clothed, and gather grass from the mountains. For he says: "Who feedeth a flock, and eateth not of its milk?"[72] Therefore the anchorite must guard this flock night and day, lest any of the lambs be caught by wild beasts or fall into the hands of thieves. If such a thing should happen in the valley, he should at once snatch it away from the mouth of the lion and the bear.[73]

Our thought about our brother is caught by wild beasts, if it feeds us with hatred; and so is our thought about a woman, if it turns about in us with shameful desire; and likewise our thought about gold and silver, if it dwells in us with greed; so also our thoughts about Divine gifts, if they graze in the mind with vainglory. The same will happen in the case of the other thoughts if they are stolen by the passions.

One must guard these "sheep" not only during the

[71] *Psalms* 22: 2 (Septuagint).
[72] *1 Corinthians* 9: 7.
[73] Cf. *1 Kings* 17: 35 (Septuagint).

day, at night also one should vigilantly protect them. For it happens that when one has shameful and evil fantasies he loses what is his own. This is the meaning of the statement of holy Joseph: "I brought not to thee a sheep which was killed by the beasts; I made good of myself the thefts of the day and the thefts of the night. I was parched with heat by day, and chilled with frost by night, and my sleep departed from my eyes."[74]

If a certain despondency should come to us from our toils, reverting a little to the rock of knowledge, let us converse with the Psalter, plucking at the strings with the virtues of knowledge. Let us feed again the sheep below Mount Sinai, in order that the God of our fathers may call us, too, out of the bush,[75] and grant to us the reasons of the signs and of the wonders.

17. Our rational nature (λογική φύσις), which became dead through wickedness, is resurrected by Christ through the contemplation of all the aeons. And His Father raises, through the knowledge of Him, the soul which has died the death of Christ. And this is the meaning of Paul's statement: "If we

[74] *Genesis* 31: 39-40 (Septuagint).
[75] *Genesis* 3.

be dead with Christ," we believe that "we shall also live with Him."[76]

18. When the mind has put off the old man and put on the man of Grace, then it shall see its own state during prayer, somewhat like sapphire of sky-blue. This state Scripture calls God's place that was seen by the elders on Mount Sinai."[77]

19. Of the unclean demons, some tempt man as man, while others disturb man as an irrational animal. The first, approaching us, introduce into us thoughts of vainglory, or pride, or envy, or accusation, which affect none of the irrational animals. The second, approaching us, arouse anger or desire that is contrary to nature. For these passions are common to us and the brutes, and are covered by our rational nature. To the thoughts that come to men as men, the Holy Spirit says; "I have said, ye are gods, and all of you are sons of the Most High; but ye shall die as men, and fall like one of the princes."[78] Whereas to those thoughts that move (in men) irrationally, what does he say? "Be ye not as the horse or as the mule, which have no understanding; whose mouth must be held in with bit and bridle, lest they come

---

[76] *2 Timothy* 2: 11.
[77] *Exodus* 24: 10 (Septuagint).
[78] *Psalms* 81: 6-7 (Septuagint).

near unto thee."[79] Now if "the soul that sinneth, it shall die,"[80] it is manifest that men die as men and are buried by men, whereas the irrational when put to death or fall, will be eaten by vultures or ravens. Some of their young call upon the Lord,[81] while others "roll themselves in blood."[82] "He that hath ears to hear let him hear."[83]

20. When one of your enemies approaches you and wounds you, and you wish to turn aside his sword, as is written, upon his heart, do as follows, as we tell you. Analyze in yourself the thought that was suggested by him, what it is, what it consists of, and what in it especially affects your mind. I mean something like this. Let us say that the thought of money was sent to you by him. Divide this thought into the mind which received it, the idea of gold, gold itself, and the passion of greed. Then ask: Which of these is sin. Is it the mind? But then how is it in the image of God? Is it the idea of God? But what intelligent person would say this? Then is gold itself sin? And for whose sake was gold created? It follows, there-

---

[79] *Psalms* 31: 9 (Septuagint).
[80] *Ezekiel* 18: 4 (Septuagint).
[81] *Psalms* 147: 9 (Septuagint).
[82] *Job* 39: 30 (Septuagint).
[83] *Matthew* 11: 15.

fore, that the cause of sin is the fourth, the passion of greed. This is neither a thing that exists as a substance, nor the idea of a thing, but a certain pleasure that is inimical to man. It springs from free will and compels the mind to use God's creatures in an evil manner. This pleasure God's law entrusts us to cut off.

Now as you are investigating these things, the thought will be destroyed, thus analyzed into its own explanation. And the demon will depart from you, your intellect having been lifted high by this knowledge. If, however, you do not want to use his sword against him, but wish first to overpower him with your sling, throw a stone out of your shepherd's small bag and meditate on the following. How is it that angels and demons approach our world, whereas we do not approach their worlds. For we cannot bring angels closer to God, neither do we choose to render demons more impure. And how was Lucifer, the morning star, thrown down to the earth?[84] He reviewed the sea like a soothing ointment, and Tartarus of the abyss as a slave, and "makes the deep boil like a brazen caldron."[85] Agitating all by his wickedness, he wants to rule all.

[84] Cf. *Isaiah* 14: 12.
[85] *Job* 41: 23-24 (Septuagint).

Meditation on these things wounds the demon and banishes his whole company. This happens, however, in the case of those who have quietly been purified and see to a certain extent the causes of the events. The impure, on the other hand, do not know how to meditate on these things. And even when they have heard from others how to overcome the enemy by a spell they will not succeed, owing to the dust and the commotion that is caused by their passions during the warfare of the demons. For it is necessary that alien company quiet down, in order that Goliath alone meet our David.[86] Similarly, let us use both the analysis and the proper form of warfare against unclean thoughts.

21. When some of the unclean thoughts have been quickly banished, let us seek the cause, whence this has happened. Did it happen because the object of the unclean thought is rare, and it is difficult to find matter for it? Or did it happen because of our present passionlessness? For example, if a certain, anchorite should happen to think of being entrusted with the spiritual rule of a city, he would not continue to hold this thought for a long time. It is an instance of the first explanation. If, however, some anchorite should

---

[86] Cf. *1 Kings* 17 (Septuagint).

actually become the spiritual leader (a bishop) of a certain city and should continue to think the way he thought before, he is blessed with passionlessness.

This method when examined will be found to apply in a similar manner to other thoughts. It is necessary to know these with a view to our zeal and power, in order that we might perceive whether we have crossed the Jordan,[87] and are near the palm-trees, or are still in the desert and are being struck by aliens.

The demon of greed seems to me to be quite varied and extraordinary as regards deceit. Often, when straightened by the extreme renunciation of a monastic, he at once pretends that he is thrifty and loves the poor. He welcomes as a very genuine host strangers who are not yet present, and sends means of service to others who are absent. He visits prisons of the city and pretends to ransom those who have been sold as slaves. Also, he suggests that one cleave to wealthy women. Again, he advises others to become obedient to persons who have a full purse.

Having thus, little by little, deceived the soul, he surrounds it with thoughts of money-making, and gives it over to the demon of vainglory. The latter introduces into the mind a multitude who praise the Lord for these good deeds that were done (in

[87] Cf. *Joshua* 3.

the form of fantasies). And gradually this demon manages to get some to talk with one another about the anchorite receiving the Priesthood. He predicts the death of the actual priest, and will not avoid it even though he should do myriads of things. Thus the miserable man, having been entangled in these thoughts, contends against those men who do not consent to his becoming a priest, while to those who consent he readily offers gifts and admits them to his presence with gratitude. Some others who disagree he turns over to the judges and orders that they be exiled from the city.

Now while these thoughts are within him and are turning about, the demon of pride suddenly comes sending continuous lightning against the air of the cell as well as winged dragons. Finally, he strives to deprive the anchorite of his wits. We, praying for the destruction of these thoughts, let us live in poverty with thanks. For we brought nothing into the world, and it is clear that we cannot carry off anything either. "Having food and raiment let us be therewith content,"[88] remembering Paul, who says: "The love of money is the root of all evil."[89]

[88] *1 Timothy* 6: 8.
[89] *1 Timothy* 6: 10.

22. All impure thoughts, lingering in us through the passions, bring down the mind to ruin and perdition. Just as the thought of bread lingers in the mind of the hungry person because of hunger, and the thought of water in the mind of the thirsty person because of thirst, so the thoughts of money and shameful thoughts that arise from foods linger because of the passions. The same will be made manifest with regard to the thoughts of vainglory and the others. For a mind that is choked with such thoughts it is not possible to stand before God and win the crown of righteousness. Drawn down by these thoughts that thrice-unhappy mind in the Gospels declined the supper of the knowledge of God.[90] Again, he who was bound hand and foot and cast into out darkness[91] had his garment woven of these thoughts, and was called not worthy of such a wedding by the person who had invited him. The wedding garment is the passionlessness (ἀπάθεια) of a rational soul, which has renounced worldly desires. In the Chapters on Prayer, the explanation was given as to why the lingering of the thoughts of things that are perceived by the senses causes the corruption of knowledge.

[90] Cf. *Luke* 14: 18.
[91] *Matthew* 22: 13.

23. Of the demons that are opposed to spiritual practices there are three who are leaders. These are followed by the whole army of aliens. These three leaders stand first in the warfare and entice the souls to vice through impure thoughts. They are the demons who are entrusted with the desires of gluttony, those who suggest the love of money, and those who call us forth to human glory. Since you desire pure prayer (καθαρὰ προσευχή), preserve anger (against the demons). And since you love chastity (σωφροσύνη), control your belly, and do not give bread to your belly to surfeit and afflict it by drinking only water. Be vigilant in prayer and keep malice far from you. Be not without words of the Holy Spirit, and knock on the doors of the Scriptures with the hands of the virtues. Then there will dawn in you passionlessness of the heart, and you will behold your mind star-like during prayer.

BY THE SAME (EVAGRIOS)

FROM THE CHAPTERS OF INNER WAKEFULNESS

1. A monk should always be alive as if he were to die tomorrow. Again, he should treat his body as if it were to live for many years. The former cuts off thoughts of desponency (ἀκηδία) and renders the monk more zealous, while the latter keeps the body sound and mantains self-restraint undiminished.

2. He who has attained knowledge and has enjoyed the pleasure that comes from it will no longer be persuaded by the demon of vainglory when he offers all the pleasures of the world. For what could he promise that is greater than that spiritual contemplation? However, so long as we have not tasted this knowledge let us devote ourselves eagerly to spiritual practices, thus showing our aim to God, that we are doing everything for the sake of knowledge (γνῶσις) of Him.

3. It is necessary to set forth the ways of the monks who have made progress, and succeed by following them. For these are many things which they have done and said well. Among these is the following statement made by one of them, that the drier

and not irregular diet, when joined with love, faster brings the monk to the harbor of passionlessness.

4. I once went at noontime to Saint Macarios burning from thirst, I asked for water to drink. And he says: Let the shade suffice. There are many at this moment who are traveling by land or water, and are lacking even this." Then, as we were discussing the subject of self-restraint, he says: "Be of good courage, my son; for I myself, during a period of twenty years did not receive to surfeit either bread, or water, or sleep, but I ate in moderation, and drank water in moderation, and leaning a little against the wall I snatched a little sleep."

5. Reading, vigils, and prayer make a wandering mind stand still. Hunger, exertion, and withdrawal from the world wither burning lust. Psalmodizing, longsuffering, and compassion stop seething anger. For what is immoderate and unseasonable is of short duration, rather harmful, not beneficial.

CHAPTER 4

BRIEF BIOGRAPHY
OF SAINT CASSIAN THE ROMAN

Whose Memory is Celebrated on February 29

Our holy Father John Cassian the Roman lived during the reign of Theodosios the Younger, and flourished around the year 431 A.D. Of the discourses which he authored, there have been placed here the one about *The Eight Thoughts* and the one about *Discrimination*, as they emit every kind of benefit and grace. They are mentioned by the most wise Photios, who in *The 157ᵗʰ Reading* says the following: "The second discourse is addressed to the same person (namely, Kastor, and bears the title *Concerning the Eight Thoughts*. It pertains to gluttony, fornication, greed, anger, sorrow, despondency, vainglory, and pride. These discourses are extremely useful for those who choose to undertake the struggle of asceticism. He also wrote a brief discourse which teaches what discrimination is, that it is greater than the other virtues, whence it is engendered—that it is rather a gift from Above—and so on."

The Church commemorates St. John Cassian on the 29th of the month of February, greatly honoring him with hymns of praise.

SAINT CASSIAN THE ROMAN

TO BISHOP KASTOR

ON THE EIGHT EVIL THOUGHTS

Having first written the discourse regarding the organization of coenobia, now, trusting in your prayers, we attempt to write concerning the eight evil thoughts (τῆς πονηρίας λογισμοί): gluttony, fornication, greed, anger, sorrow, despondency, vainglory, and pride.

1. CONCERNING RESTRAINT OF THE BELLY

First, I shall speak to you about restraint of the belly (ἐγκράτεια γαστρός), which is opposed to gluttony (γαστριμαργία), about the manner of fasting, and about the quality (ποιότης) and quantity (ποσότης) of foods. I shall speak about these not from myself, but from what we have received from our holy Fathers. They have not handed down one rule with regard to fasting, or one manner of partaking of foods, or the same measure (for all). The reason for this is the fact that all do not have the same strength, either because

ST. JOHN CASSIAN THE ROMAN

of difference in age, or because of disease, or because of better bodily habits. However, they have handed to all a single, universal aim: to avoid excess and to shun satiety of the belly. They found that daily fasting (in the sense of reducing the number of daily meals) is better than fasting that consists in eating every three or four days, or a week. For they say that he who extends the fast excessively often afterward eats excessively. Consequently, at times excessive fasting results in weakness of the body, and it becomes lazier with regard to spiritual activities. At times, the body, weighed down by the large quantity of food, causes despondency and languor to the soul. Again, the Fathers tried and found that living on vegetables or pulses alone is not suitable for all, and that not all can live on dry bread alone. And they said that one individual may eat two pounds of bread and still feel hungry, whereas another may eat only one pound or six ounces and feel satisfied.

Therefore, as I said earlier, the holy Fathers gave one rule for self-restraint, not to be deceived by satiety of the belly, and not to be lured by the pleasure of the larynx. For it is not only the difference in the quality of the foods, but also the quantity that kindles the fiery darts of fornication. For when the belly is full of any food whatsoever, it produces the seed of dissipation. Again, it is not only the excessive amount of wine that causes drunkenness to the mind, but also the excess of water. The excess of every kind of food dulls the mind and makes it sleepy. The catastrophe of the Sodomites was not caused by the debauchery of wine and of various foods, but "fullness of bread," according to the Prophet.[1]

Bodily sickness is not opposed to purity of the heart, when we give to the body what the sickness requires, and not what pleasure desires. The use of foods should be made to the degree that is necessary for supporting our life, not in order to be enslaved to impulses and desires. The partaking of food in moderation and according to reason contributes to the health of the body. Then it does not deprive one of holiness. The definition and precise rule of self-restraint that has been handed down by the Fathers is this: to stop eating before we reach the point of satiety. And the Apostle, when he said: "Make no provision for the flesh, to fulfill the lusts thereof,"[2] did not oppose the necessary taking care of the body, but the pleasure-loving care.

Besides, for the perfect purity of the soul, self-re-

[1] *Ezekiel* 16:49.

straint with regard to foods is not enough, the other virtues must be present. Humility and obedience and the subduing of the body are of great benefit. The avoidance of greed—not only the non-possession of money, but also freedom from desire for them—are conducive to purity of the soul. The avoidance of anger, of sorrow, of vainglory, of pride, all this is conducive to the general purity of the soul. The partial purity of the soul is especially effected by self-restraint and fasting. It is impossible for one who has his belly satiated to mentally wage war against the spirit of fornication. Therefore, let our first struggle be to master our belly and to subjugate our body, not only by means of fasting, but also by means of vigils, and toil, and reading, and by concentrating our heart on the fear of hell and on the longing of the Kingdom of Heaven.

2. ON THE SPIRIT OF FORNICATION AND THE DESIRE OF THE FLESH

Our second struggle is against the spirit of fornication (τὸ πνεῦμα τῆς πορνείας) and the desire of the flesh (ἐπιθυμία τῆς σαρκός), which desire begins to annoy man from an early age. This struggle is great and difficult, having two sides. For whereas in

the case of the other defects of character the fight is
only in the soul, this is twofold, both in the soul and
in the body, and for this reason we must undertake
a twofold struggle.[2] Bodily fasting does not suffice
for the acquisition of perfect chastity and true purity.
There must also be contrition of the heart, extended
prayer to God, and frequent study of the Scriptures,
fatigue, and manual work. These are capable of re-
pulsing fickle impulses of the soul, and to call it back
from shameful fantasies. Above all, humility of the
soul contributes to this. Without humility neither
fornication nor any other passion can be overcome.
First of all then one must guard the soul most attentively from unclean thoughts.[3] For, as the Lord has
said, "out of the heart proceed evil thoughts, murders, adulteries, fornications,"[4] and so on. Fasting
has been ordained not only for the subjugation of
the body, but also for the sake of watchfulness of
the mind, lest being darkened by too much food, it
become weak in the guarding of the thoughts. It is
necessary to exercise great diligence with regard to
bodily fasting, but also in watching our thoughts at-

[2] *Romans* 13:14.
[3] *Proverbs* 4:23.
[4] *Matthew* 15:19.

tentively and in spiritual meditation. Without these
it is impossible to rise to the height of true chastity and purity. It is proper therefore for us first "to
clean," as our Lord says, "that which is within the
cup and the platter, that the outside of them may
be clean also."[5] For precisely this reason, if there is
in us the earnestness, according to the Apostle "to
strive lawfully and be crowned,"[6] having defeated
the impure spirit of fornication, let us not trust in our
own power and askesis, but in the help of our Master
God. For man does not cease being fought by this
spirit, until he truly comes to believe that not by his
own endeavor, or his own toil, but by God's protection and help he is freed from this disease and rises
to the height of purity. This is something above nature, and somehow he who has trampled upon the
excitements of the flesh and its pleasures transcends
the body. Therefore, it is impossible for man (to put
it thus) to fly with his own wings to this sublime and
heavenly prize of holiness and become an imitator
of Angels, unless the grace of God lifts him up from
the earth and mud. For by no other virtue are men,
while united with flesh, made more similar to Angels

[5] *Matthew* 23:26
[6] *2 Timothy* 6:10

than they are by chastity. By it, while dwelling on the earth, they "have their commonwealth in Heaven," according to the Apostle.[7]

A token that we have perfectly acquired this virtue is the fact that we have no image of shameful fantasy during our sleep. For although the appearance of such an image is not considered a sin, it is evidence that the soul is sick and has not been freed from the passion. Therefore, we must believe that the shameful fantasies that appear to us during sleep are evidence of our antecedent sloth and of the sickness in us. The sickness which is hidden in the secret parts of the soul is made manifest by emissions during our sleep. For this reason the Physician of our souls placed the medicine in the secret parts of the soul, where He knew that there exist the causes of our sickness, saying: "Whosoever looketh on a woman to lust after her hath committed adultery."[8] He corrected not so much the curious and lustful eyes, as the soul, which has its dwelling place in us and makes evil use of the eyes, which God gave for the good of man. For this reason the wise Proverb does not say: "By all means guard your eyes," but says:

[7] *Philippians* 3:20
[8] *Matthew* 5:28

"By all means guard your heart."[9] That is, place the medicine of attention upon your heart, which uses the eyes for whatever it wishes.

Let, then, the following be the guarding of our heart. When there comes to our mind a memory of a woman, which sprang from diabolic cunning, whether it be of the mother, the sister, or of other devout women, let us at once banish it, lest by our lingering on it the evil deceiver roll down our mind and throw it down a precipice, to shameful and harmful thoughts. The commandment that was given by God to the first man enjoins to watch the head of the serpent,[10] that is, the beginnings of harmful thoughts, by means of which the serpent endeavors to creep into our soul. For the acceptance of the head, which is the suggestion of a thought, will result the acceptance of the rest of the body of the serpent, which consists in assent (συγκατάθεσις) to the pleasure. And this will lead the mind to the illicit act.

It is proper, as it is written, "Every morning I will destroy all the sinners of the earth,"[11] that is, it is proper, with the light of knowledge, to discriminate and destroy sinful thoughts from the earth, which

---

[9] *Proverbs*: 4:23
[10] Cf. *Genesis* 3:15
[11] *Psalm* 100:8

is our heart, according to the teaching of our Lord. And while the sons of Babylon are still infants—that is, evil thoughts—"to dash them against the stone,"[12] which is Christ. For if, through your ascent, they grow up into manhood, it will not be possible to defeat them without strenuous efforts.

In addition to the preceding sayings from Holy Scripture, it is good to remember sayings of the holy Fathers. Saint Basil, Bishop of Cappadocia, has said: "I do not know a woman and I am not a virgin." He knew that the gift of virginity is not attained merely by bodily abstinence from a woman, as much as by holiness and purity of the soul, which naturally is achieved with fear of God. The Fathers also say this, that we cannot acquire the virtue of purity perfectly unless we previously acquire true humility in our heart, or true knowledge, so long as the passion of fornication remains settled in the secret parts of the soul.

In order to show also from the Apostle how great an achievement chastity is, we shall recall one of his sayings and stop: "Follow peace with all men, and holiness, without which no man shall see the Lord."[13]

[12] *Psalm* 136:9
[13] *Hebrews* 12:14

That he is referring to our topic is evident from what he goes on to say: "No fornicator or profane person, as Esau."[14] So, in proportion as the achievement of holiness is heavenly and angelic, it is fought against by means of greater intrigues of the enemies (the demons). For this reason we must endeavor not only to cultivate self-restraint of the body, but also compunction of the heart and frequent prayers accompanied by sighs, in order that by means of the cool water of the presence of the Holy Spirit we might extinguish the fire in the furnace of our flesh, which the Babylonian King daily ignites by means of the excitement of lust.[15]

Besides these, an exceedingly great weapon for us in this war is godly vigil. For just as daytime watchfulness is conducive to nighttime holiness, so godly nighttime vigil is conducive to daytime purity of the soul.

3. ON AVARICE

Our third struggle is against the spirit of avarice (φυλαργυρία). It is an alien war and outside hu-

[14] *Hebrews* 12:16
[15] Cf. *Daniel* 3:19 ff

man nature, occasioned by lack of faith in a monk.
For other passions—anger and lust—seem to have
their beginning from the body, and in a certain way
to be innate, and therefore, a long period of time is
required for overcoming them. The disease of avarice, on the other hand, coming from outside, can be
banished more easily, if it be treated with diligence
and attention. However, if it is neglected, it becomes
more pernicious than the other passions and more
difficult to get rid of. For it is the root of all the evils,
according to the Apostle.[16]

Let us reflect as follows. The natural movements
of the body are observed not only in children, in
whom there is no judgment about good and evil,
and in suckling infants, which do not have even a
trace of pleasure, but give signs that they have by nature movement in their flesh. Similarly, the center of
anger is observed in infants when they are aroused
against those who grieve them. I say these things not
in order to blame nature as the cause of sin—not at
all; but in order to show that anger and desire, even
though they were united with human nature by the
Creator for a good end, they decline from the state
according to nature to a state that is contrary to na-

---

[16] *1 Timothy* 6:10

ture, as a result of sloth. The movement of the body was given by the Creator for the begetting of children and the continuation of human species, not for fornication. And the movement of anger has been given by Him for contributing to our salvation; for being angry at badness and not for being angry at our fellow men. Therefore, if we use these in evil ways, this does not mean that human nature is sinful or that our Creator is to be blamed. Just as we do not blame the person who gave an iron tool to someone for a necessary and beneficial use, if the recipient used it for murder.

We have said these things in order to show that the passion of avarice does not originate from the nature of man, but solely from very bad and corrupt deliberate choice. This disease, when it finds the soul at the beginning of renunciation lukewarm and unbelieving, suggests to it certain pretexts which are in appearance just and reasonable for withholding some of the things which he has acquired. It tells the monk that he is going to have old age of long duration and bodily sickness, and that the necessaries provided by the coenobium are not going to be sufficient for a sick person, or even for one who is in good health; and that here they do not provide adequate care for the sick, but an altogether neglectful one; and that if he does not hide gold he will die a miserable death. Finally, it suggests that he will not be able to remain long at the monastery, owing to the heavy work and the austereness of the abbot.

When it has led the mind astray, by means of such thoughts, to acquire at least one denarius, it persuades him to learn, secretly from the abbot, a handicraft, whereby he may be able to acquire the money which he so much desires. Thus, by secret hopes it deceives the wretched one, suggesting to him to profit from the handicraft and the comfort and freedom from care that will result from it. Having surrendered himself to the thought of profit, he pays no attention to other evil: neither the madness of anger that will result if he should suffer some loss, nor the darkness of sorrow if he should fail in his hope of profit. But just as for others their belly becomes their god, so for him gold becomes his god. This is why the blessed Apostle called avarice not only the root of evils,[17] but also idolatry.[18]

So let us see to what great badness this disease pulls down man as to lead him to put idolatry into his mind. Having drawn his mind away from the love of God, the avaricious man loves the likenesses of man

---

[17] *1 Timothy* 6:10
[18] *1 Timothy* 6:10

engraved on gold coins. The mind of the monk, having been darkened by such thoughts and growing worse, cannot have obedience at all. Instead, he is indignant, thinks that he is suffering unjustly, and for every task he grumbles, he contradicts, without any piety. Like an unyielding horse, he heads for the precipice. He is not satisfied with the daily food, and protests that he cannot endure these things indefinitely. He says that God is not only there, that salvation is not to be found only there, and that if he leaves that monastery he will not lose his soul. Having in support of this corrupt opinion his treasured money, he feels these as wings, and dwells on the thought of leaving the monastery. Therefore, he responds proudly and rudely to all the orders that are given to him, and considers himself as an alien and outsider. And if he sees in the monastery something that needs repair, he is negligent and scornful, and is disdainful of everything that is done.

Then he looks for pretexts whereby he will become angry or sorrowful, in order that he might not appear light-minded, and to have left the monastery without reason. If he is capable of getting someone out of the monastery, by means of whispering and vain talk, he will not refrain from doing this, too, wishing to have a collaborator.

Thus afire by the fire of his own money, the avaricious individual will never be able to be at peace in a monastery, or to live under a rule.

When the demon, like a wolf, seizes him from the fold and separates him from the flock, ready to devour him, then brings him to the point to do at his cell day and night with great eagerness those things which at the coenobium he was lazy to do at definite hours. And he does not allow him to observe the rules that pertain to the prayers, to the fasts, to the vigils. And having bound him to the mania of avarice, persuades him to have all his zeal turned to his handicraft.

There are three forms of this disease, all of which the Divine Scriptures and the teachings of the Fathers forbid. One of them is that which makes those who were poor while in the world to strive to acquire now those things which they did not have. Another one consists in making those who once renounced money to regret that act, suggesting to them that they ask for the money which they had offered to God. The third is that which, having bound the monk with unbelief and lukewarmness, does not allow him to be deprived completely of things, reminiscent of poverty and suggesting to him unbelief in God's providence. Thus he proves him an apostate of his own promises which he gave when he renounced the world.

We found the examples of these three kinds of disease of the soul condemned in Divine Scripture. Thus, Gehazi, because he desired to acquire the money which he did not have before, failed to receive the gift of prophecy, which his teacher wanted to leave to him as an inheritance. And instead of a blessing he received leprosy, through the curse of the Prophet.[19] And Judas, who wanted to take money, which previously he had renounced, having followed Christ, not only slipped and fell from the choir of the Apostles, through his betrayal of the Lord, and even ended his life in the flesh with a violent death.[20] And Ananias and Sapheira, having kept some of the money which they possessed, were punished with death by the Apostolic mouth.[21] And the great Moses, in the *Deuteronomy* enjoins in a mystical manner to those who promise to renounce the world, and through the fear of lack of faith are bound by earthly things; "If there is someone who is frightened and timid, let him not go out to the war, but instead go to his home and stay there, lest he cause his brothers to be themselves frightened."[22]

[19] *4 Kings* 5:25.
[20] *Matthew* 27:4.
[21] *Acts of the Apostles* 5:5, 10.
[22] *Deuteronomy* 20:8.

Is there a surer and clearer testimony that those who renounce the world must renounce it completely, and with resolve proceed to the war, and not, by setting out with a languid and corrupt will turn away others from Evangelical perfection, and imbue them with timidity.

That which is well said in Divine Scripture: "It is more blessed to give than to receive,"[23] is badly interpreted by those who are eager to deceive themselves and to justify their avarice, misinterpreting the saying and the teaching of Christ, Who says: "If thou wilt be perfect, go and sell what thou hast, and give to the poor, and thou shalt have treasure in Heaven: and come and follow Me."[24] They judge that having your own wealth and giving from this to the poor is more blessed than non-possession of property. Let such persons realize that they have not yet renounced the world, and have not attained to monastic perfection, since they are ashamed to become poor for the sake of Christ, like the Apostle (Paul), and with the work of their hands to support themselves as well as those who are in need,[25] and with deeds to fulfill the monastic promise, and to be glorified like the Apostle.

[23] *Acts* 20:35.
[24] *Matthew* 19:21.
[25] *Acts of the Apostles* 20:34.

Having given away the old wealth, let them struggle, together with Paul, "in hunger and thirst, in cold
and nakedness."[26] For if the same Apostle knew that
the old wealth was more useful for the perfection of
man, he would not have despised it, for he was, according to his own testimony, a notable Roman citi-
zen.[27] And the Christians in Jerusalem were selling
their homes and farms, and were placing the money received from these at the feet of the Apostles.
They would not have done this if they knew that
the Apostles thought that it was better to be fed by
expending this money and not that earned by their
own toil and the contributions of the Gentiles. The
Apostle teaches about this more clearly by what he
writes to the Romans: "But now I go unto Jerusalem
to minister unto the saints.... It hath pleased them
verily; and their debtors they are."[28] And he himself,
when he was in fetters and in prison many times, and
was harassed by long journeys—something which
hindered him from working with his hands, as he
was accustomed, for getting his necessities—teaches
that he received these from his brethren who came
from Macedonia, saying: "That which was lacking to

[26] *2 Corinthians* 11:27.
[27] *Acts of the Apostles* 22:25.
[28] *Romans* 15; 25; 27.

me the brethren which came from Macedonia supplied."[29] And to the Philippians he wrote: "Now ye Philippians know also, that when I departed from Macedonia, no church communicated with me as concerning giving and receiving, but ye only. For even in Thessaloniki ye sent once and again unto my necessity."[30]

Let then these, according to the opinion of the avaricious, be considered more blessed than the Apostle, because they provided to him the necessities out of their own belongings. But no one will reach the point of such foolishness to dare say this.

Therefore, if we wish to follow the Gospel commandment and the whole Church founded from the beginning on the Apostles, let us not follow our own opinions, and let us not misinterpret what has been well said. And having disregarded our lukewarm and faithless opinion, let us espouse the strictness (ἀκρίβεια) of the Gospel. For then we shall be able to follow in the footsteps of the Fathers, and never abandon the wisdom of the coenobium, and to truly renounce the world.

It is good in this connection to recall the saying of a Saint, in particular of Basil, Bishop of Caesarea of

[29] *2 Corinthians* 11:9.
[30] *Philippians* 4:15.

Cappadocia. It is said that he once made the following statement to a member of a senate who had renounced the world in a lukewarm manner and had kept some of his money: "You have lost the member of the senate and you have not become a monk."

It is necessary, therefore, to remove from one's soul the root of all the evils, which is avarice, knowing with certainty that when the root remains, branches easily grow. To achieve this virtue is something difficult, if one does not live in a coenobium. For in it we are free from cares even with regard to necessaries.

Having before us the condemnation of Ananias and Sapphira, let us shudder when we think of keeping something of our old belongings. Similarly, fearing the example of Gehazi, who because of his avarice was surrendered to eternal leprosy, let us avoid gathering money, which we did not have even in the world. Again, thinking of the end of Judas by hanging, let us fear taking back something which we despised when we renounced the world.

In addition to these things, always having in mind the unknown time of our death, that it might come at an hour when we are not expecting our Lord to come and find our conscience stained by avarice, and say to us what was said in the Gospel to that rich man: "Thou fool, this night thy soul shall be required of thee: then whose shall those things be, which thou hast acquired?"[31]

4. ON ANGER

Our fourth struggle is against the spirit of anger (ὀργή) and the necessity, with God's help, to extirpate from the depth of our soul its death-causing virus. For when this is seated in our heart, and blinds the eyes of the heart by its dark agitations, we can neither acquire discrimination of what is to our (spiritual) interests, nor attain to spiritual knowledge, nor gain perfect possession of a good thought, nor to become participants of true life, nor will our mind become receptive of the contemplation of the Divine and true Light. For Scripture says: "My eye was disturbed by anger."[32] Neither will we become participants of Divine wisdom, even if we are regarded by all others as very wise. For it is written: "Anger resteth in the bosom of fools."[33] Nor will we be able to acquire the salvific counsels of discernment, even if we are regarded by men as prudent. For it is written: "Anger destroyeth even the prudent."[34] Nor will

[31] *Luke* 12:20.
[32] *Psalm* 7:9.
[33] *Ecclesiastes* 7:8.
[34] *Proverbs* 15:1.

we be able to render justice with a dispassionate heart, for it is written: "The wrath of man worketh not the righteousness of God."[35] Nor can we acquire the decorum and decency that are praised by all, for it is written: "An irascible man is not decorous."[36]

Therefore, he who wants to attain perfection, and desires to engage in the spiritual struggle lawfully, must be free of every fault related to anger and alien to it. And let him listen to what the vessel of election himself (the Apostle Paul) orders: "Let all bitterness, and wrath, and anger, and clamor, and evil speaking be put away from you, with all malice."[37] When he says "all," he leaves us no pretext for anger as either necessary or reasonable. Therefore, he who wants to correct his brother when he sins, or to impose upon him penance, should be careful to remain calm, lest wishing to heal another person, he should become sick himself. Then, the Gospel saying will apply to him: "Physician, heal thyself."[38] Also, the following will apply: "Why beholdest thou the mote that is in thy brother's eye, but considerest not the beam that is in thine own eye?"[39] For from whatever reason the

[35] *James* 1:20.
[36] *Proverbs* 11:25.
[37] *Ephesians* 4:31.
[38] *Luke* 4:23.
[39] *Matthew* 7:3.

movement of anger becomes excited, it renders the eye of the soul blind, and does not let the soul see the Sun of Righteousness. He who places on his eyes covers made of gold or lead obstructs sight, and the preciousness of gold makes no difference at all to the blindness. Similarly, from whatever cause, supposedly reasonable, or unreasonable, anger is kindled, the vision of the soul is darkened.

We use anger according to nature (κατὰ φύσιν) only when we direct it to passionate and pleasure-loving thoughts. Thus, the Prophet teaches: "Get angry and do not sin."[40] That is, arouse anger against your own passions and against evil thoughts, and do not sin by doing what they suggest. And clearly, this is the meaning of what follows: "What ye say in your hearts, say on your bed and feel contrition." That is, when evil thoughts come to your heart, after expelling them by means of anger against them, being in the quietness if the soul as on a bed, repent with contrition. Blessed Paul agrees with this, using this testimony and adding: "Let not the sun go down upon your wrath. Neither give place to the devil."[41] That is, do not dispose thus the Sun of Righteousness, Christ, provoking Him by assenting

[40] *Psalm* 4:5.
[41] *Ephesians* 4:26-27.

to base thoughts, to depart from your heart, and following His departure, the devil find a place in you. About this Sun, God says through His Prophet: "The Sun of Righteousness shall arise with the healing in His wings."[42] If we take this saying literally, it is not forgivable to retain anger even until sunset.

What shall we say about this? We keep the ferocity and madness of the passion of anger not only until the setting of the sun, but prolong it for many days. We do not express our anger by means of words, but through our silence with one another we increase the venom of rancor that leads to our destruction. We ignore that we must avoid not only overt anger, but also anger in the mind, in order that the mind might not be darkened by the darkness of rancor, and fall from the light of knowledge and discernment, and be deprived of the indwelling of the Holy Spirit. This is why in the Gospels the Lord enjoins that one leave his gift before the altar and be reconciled with his brother,[43] for it is not possible for it to be accepted when anger and rancor are present in us. And the Apostle teaches us this when he says: "Pray unceasingly,"[44] and at every place "lifting up holy

[42] *Malachias* 4:2
[43] *Matthew* 5:23
[44] *1 Thessalonians* 5:17

hands, without wrath and doubting."[45] Therefore, either we must never pray, and thereby be accountable for ignoring the precept of the Apostle, or we must strive to observe it, praying without anger and rancor. And because often our brethren are saddened or disturbed by us, we are indifferent, saying that we are not the cause of their sadness, the Physician of souls, wishing to uproot the pretexts from our souls, enjoins us to leave the gift and be reconciled with our brother, not only if we are grieved against our brother, but also if he is grieved against us, whether justly or unjustly, healing him through apology, and then offering the gift. But why should we dwell on the precepts of the Gospels, when we can learn these from the Old Testament, too. Although its teaching is regarded as being not so strict, it says the following: "Thou shalt not hate thy brother in thy heart;"[46] and "The ways of the rancorous lead to death."[47] Here not only overt rancor is prohibited, but also rancor which we harbor in the mind. Therefore, it is proper for those who follow the Divine Laws to struggle with all their power against the spirit of anger and against the disease which is inside us. We

[45] *1 Timothy* 2:8
[46] *Leviticus* 19:17
[47] *Proverbs* 12:28

must not arouse our anger against men. We must not withdraw from the world and live in solitude, for there the causes that excite our anger. Thus the virtue of longsuffering will easily be acquired. Due to the fact that we are proud and do not want to blame ourselves, and attribute to ourselves and to our sloth the causes of our agitation, we desire departure from our brethren. As long as we attribute the causes of our disease to them, it is impossible for us to attain to the perfection of longsuffering.

The chief thing, therefore, for our correction and peace lies not in the forbearance of our neighbor towards us, but in our own forbearance towards our neighbor. When we avoid the struggle for forbearance, and seek the desert and being alone, whatever uncured passions of ours we take there remain hidden and not removed. The desert and withdrawal, in the case of those who have not freed themselves from passions, not only preserves the passions, but also conceals them. And it does not let them know by which passion they are stirred. On the contrary, it instills in them the fantasy of virtue and persuades them that they have achieved forbearance and humility, so long as there is no one present to irritate them and test them. And when an occasion arises which moves them and puts them to the test, at once the indwelling passions, like unbridled horses, leap up. And having been fed by the long quiet and idleness, they draw the rider towards destruction in a stronger and fiercer manner. For the passions in us grow fiercer when the discipline that is provided by men is absent. Even the shadow of patience and forbearance, which we fancy that we have when we mingle with others, we lose by our neglect of discipline and by solitude. Just as poisonous beasts that rest in their nests in the wilderness show their mania when someone approaches them, so in like manner, impassioned men, being calm, not through virtue, but owing to the quiet of the desert, vomit venom when they grasp someone who approaches them and irritates them. For this reason those who aspire to acquire the perfection of meekness must make every endeavor to avoid getting angry, not only towards men, but also against animals and against inanimate things. I recall that when I dwelt in the desert I got angry against a reed because I did not like its thickness or its thinness. Also, I got angry with a piece of wood, when I wanted to cut it and was not able to do this quickly. Again, I got angry with a stone of the type that emit fire (when struck), and it did not emit fire at once. Anger had grown so strong, that it directed itself even against inanimate things.

Therefore, if we wish to receive the blessing of the Lord, we must avoid, as we have said, not only overt anger, but also anger that we harbor in the mind. For to restrain the mouth at the time of anger and not utter furious words does not benefit so much as does the purification of the heart from rancor and avoiding harboring in the mind evil thoughts against our brother.

The Gospel teaching enjoins that we cut off the roots of sins, even if we have cut off their fruits. For if anger has been cut off from the heart, there will arise neither overt hatred, nor overt malice. For it has been said that he who hates his brother is a mankiller. He kills his brother in the disposition of his mind. Men do not see his blood shed by a sword, but God considers the mind and the disposition of hatred. He awards to each individual either crowns or punishments, not only for his overt acts, but also for his thoughts and intentions. As the Prophet says, "I come to gather their deeds and their thoughts."[48] And the Apostle says: "Their thoughts accusing or excusing one another, in the day when God shall judge the secrets of man."[49] The Lord Himself, teaching us that we ought to put away anger, says in the

[48] *Sirach* 35:22.
[49] *Romans* 2:15-16.

Gospels: "Whosoever is angry with his brother shall
be liable to Judgment."[50] This is what is said in the
precise editions of the Gospel. The expression "angry without cause" is an addition that was inserted.
This is evident from the preceding intention of the
Holy Scripture. For the aim of the Lord is that we
by all means exclude the spark of anger, and not to
harbor in ourselves a pretext for anger, in order that
we might not have a pretext for later falling into irrational anger.

The perfect therapy of the disease of anger is this:
that we believe are justified to initiate anger neither for just reasons, nor for unjust reasons. For the
spirit of anger darkens the mind, so that there will
be found in us neither the light of discernment, nor
a confirmation of right choice, of just conduct. Nor
will it be possible for our soul to be a temple of the
Holy Spirit. For the spirit of anger darkens our mind
and dominates it.

Finally, we must have before our mind, every day,
that the time of our death is unknown, and to guard
ourselves from anger. And we should realize that
neither temperance, nor the renunciation of all material things, nor fasting, nor vigils benefit us if we

---

[50] *Matthew* 5:22.

are under the power of anger and hatred. We shall be found guilty at Judgment.

5. ON SORROW

Our fifth struggle is that against the spirit of sorrow, which darkens the soul and cuts it off all spiritual contemplation, and hinders it in every kind of good work. For when this evil spirit grasps the soul and darkens it completely, it does not allow the soul to perform its prayers with eagerness, or to persist in the benefit of sacred readings. It does not tolerate one's being gentle and disposed to be contrite in relation to his brothers. It instills hatred towards all pursuits and even to the very promise of life. And plainly, sorrow confounds all the salvific deliberations of the soul, and paralyzes the vigor and fortitude of the soul, and renders it foolish and disoriented, having bound it with the thought of despair. For this reason, if our goal is to fight the spiritual fight and be victorious, with God's help, over the spirits of evil, let us guard our heart with all watchfulness[51] from the spirit of sorrow. Just as moths eat up fabrics and worms eat up wood, in the same way sorrow eats

[51] Cf. *Proverbs* 4:29.

up the soul of man. Sorrow persuades it to avoid every meeting, barring the acceptance of counsels from genuine friends, and not even permitting a good or peaceful reply to be transmitted to them. Having seized the whole soul, it fills it with bitterness and despondency (ἀκηδία).

It suggests to it to flee from men, as being the cause of the agitation within it. And it does not allow it to realize that it has this disease produced not from the outside, but from within. The disease is made manifest when one learns to observe temptations. For never will a man be harmed by another, except when he has hidden with himself the causes of the passions.

For this reason the Creator and Physician of souls, He Who alone knows exactly the wounds of the soul, does not enjoin that one abandon association with others, but to cut off the causes of vice. And to know that the health of the soul is something that is not achieved by separating oneself from men, but by association with virtuous men and by spiritual training. Therefore, when for seemingly reasonable pretexts we abandon our brethren, it means that we have not cut off the promptings of sorrow, but have only changed them. We stir up the promptings of the interior disease by means of other things.

Therefore, let our whole warfare be against the interior passions. For when these have been cast out of the heart through the Grace and synergy (συνεργεία) of God, we shall easily dwell not only with human beings, but even with the wild animals, according to the saying of blessed Job: "And the beasts of the field shall be at peace with thee."[52]

Antecedently, it is necessary to struggle against the spirit of sorrow that instills despair in the soul, that we banish it from our heart. This spirit did not permit Cain to repent after he had killed his brother; nor Judas, after the betrayal of the Lord.

Let us cultivate only that sorrow which consists in repentance for our sins, done with good hope. About this the Apostle said: "Godly sorrow worketh repentance to salvation not to be repented of; but the sorrow of the world worketh death."[53]

For Godly sorrow, nourishing the soul with the hope given by repentance, is mixed with joy. Therefore it renders man eager and obedient with reference to every good work: accessible, humble, gentle, forbearing, and patient with regard to good effort and to trouble that happen. From this are

[52] *Job* 5:23.
[53] *2 Corinthians* 7:10.

known the fruits of the Holy Spirit in man, namely, joy, love, peace, longsuffering, goodness, faith, self-restraint.[54]

By the opposed sorrow we come to a knowledge of the fruits of evil spirits. These are: despondency, impatience, anger, hatred, objection, despair, and laziness with regard to prayer. This sorrow we must avoid, as we avoid fornication, avarice, anger, and the rest of the passions. This sorrow is cured through prayer, hope in God, study of divine sayings, and association with devout men.

6. DESPONDENCY

Our sixth struggle is against the spirit of despondency (ἀκηδία). This is connected with, and acts together with, the spirit of sorrow. This demon is dreadful and grave, and is ever waging war against the monks. He attacks the monk at the sixth hour, and instills in him weakness and horror, and hatred towards the place, the brethren who dwell with him there, towards every activity, and towards the reading of the Divine Scriptures, suggesting to him even thoughts of going elsewhere; and that if he does not

[54] *Galatians* 5: 22.

betake himself to other places, all his efforts and time will be in vain.

In addition to all these things, this demon arouses hunger around the sixth hour, such as did not rise in one after a three days fast, or as a result of a very long walk, or very heavy work.

Then, this demon instills in one thoughts that he cannot free himself from this depressing disease except by going out continually to meet brethren and benefit thereby, or by visiting the sick. If he cannot deceive him in these ways, this demon sinks him in very deep sleep and thereby becomes more powerful. He cannot be overcome except by means of prayer, by the avoidance of idle talk, by meditation on divine sayings, and by patience in the time of temptations.

If he does not find the monk overcome by means of these weapons, he directs his arrows so as to render him an indolent roamer, visiting many monasteries and looking around where there are meals and drinking. For the mind of one who is despondent occupies itself with fantasies about such things. Through these, the demon binds him to worldly things. And gradually he lures this individual to such harmful preoccupations, until he completely casts him out of the monastic vocation. Divine Paul, knowing thoroughly this very grave disease, and wishing, as a wise doctor, to draw out of our souls the root of such preoccupations, points out the causes that engender them, saying: "Now we command you, brethren, in the name of our Lord Jesus Christ, that ye withdraw yourselves from every brother that walketh disorderly, and not after the tradition which he received from us. For yourselves know how ye ought to follow us; for we behaved not ourselves disorderly among you; neither did we eat any man's bread for nought; but wrought with labor and travail night and day, that we might not be chargeable to any of you; not because we have not power, but to make ourselves an example unto you to follow us. For even when we were with you, this we commanded you, that if any would not work, neither should he eat. For we hear that there are some who walk among you disorderly, working not at all, but are busybodies. Now them that are such we command and exhort by our Lord Jesus Christ, that with quietness they work and eat their own bread."[55]

Let us also listen to what the Apostle points out to be the causes of despondency. Idleness is one of the chief. It leads to disorderliness, and this to much badness. For he who is disorderly is also impious

[55] 2 *Thessalonians* 3:6-12.

and impertinent in speech, and ready to use abusive language. Therefore, he is inept for quietude and a slave of despondency. Therefore, the Apostle enjoins that we avoid such persons, that is, to separate ourselves from them as from a plague. They are proud and despisers of the Apostolic traditions and abolishers of them.

Again he says: "Neither did we eat any man's bread for nought, but wrought with labor and travail night and day."[56] The teacher of the nations, the herald of the Gospel, who ascended as far as the third heaven, who said that "the Lord hath ordained that they who preach the Gospel should live of the Gospel,"[57] yet he "wrought with labor and travail night and day" in order not to burden someone.

What then are we to do, we who take no care for work and seek bodily rest? We who have not been entrusted with the preaching of the Gospel, nor with the care of the churches, but only with the care of our own soul?

Then the Apostle, showing clearer the harm that results from idleness, speaks of: doing no work at all, but only examining curiously. For idleness results in

[56] *2 Thessalonians* 3:8.
[57] *1 Corinthians* 9:14.

curiosity; and from curiosity, disorder; and from disorder, every vice. Presenting the therapy of these, he
says: "To these we enjoin: Working with quietness,
let them eat their own bread."[58] And speaking more
sternly, he says: "If any would not work, neither
should he eat."[59]

Instructed in these Apostolic orders, the Egyptian
holy Fathers at no time permit the monks to be idle,
especially the younger ones. They know that through
the patience of work they banish despondency, pro-
cure their food, and help the needy. They work not
only for their own needs, but also provide for strangers, for the poor, and for those in prison. They believe that this benevolence becomes a holy sacrifice
that is welcome to God. The holy Fathers also say
that he who works often fights against a demon, who
is grieved by him; whereas he who is idle is taken
captive by myriads of evil spirits.

It is good to add to the preceding something that
was said to me by a very distinguished father, Abba
Moses. I had dwelt for a period of time in the desert
and was bothered by despondency. I visited him and
told him that the day before I was seriously troubled

---

[58] 2 *Thessalonians* 3:12.
[59] 2 *Thessalonians* 3:10.

by despondency, and was weakened very much. I would not have been freed from it if I had not gone to Abba Paul. With regard to this, Abba Moses said: "Have courage. You were not freed from despondency, but rather you surrendered to it as an addict. Know that henceforth it will combat you more severely as a deserter, unless you strive to overthrow it by means of patience, prayer, and work with your hands."

7. ON VAINGLORY

Our seventh struggle is against the spirit of vainglory (κενοδοξία). This is a multiform and very subtle passion, and is not quickly apprehended, even by him who has it. The suggestions of the other passions are more evident, and the battle against them is somehow easier. The soul detects the enemy, and by opposition and prayer straightway overthrows him. Vainglory, on the other hand, having many forms, as was said, is difficult to overcome. For in every vocation, in speech, in word, in silence, in deed, in vigil, in fasting, in prayer, in reading, in quietness, and in longsuffering, it endeavors to strike the soldier of Christ. For if it cannot deceive someone and make him vain by means of luxurious dress, it undertakes to tempt by means of shabby dress. And whomever it can not render haughty through honors, it lifts up to the loss of all sense through pretended dishonor. And whomever it cannot persuade to be vainglorious through learned speech, it lures him through silence to pretend to be a quiet person. And whoever it cannot persuade through luxurious food to become languid, he attracts to praise through fasting.

And generally, every activity, every vocation, provides for this cunning demon a pretext for warfare. In addition to the preceding, it suggests office. For I recall a certain monk, at the time when I dwelt at a skete, who went to the cell of a certain brother to visit him. When he was close to the door, he heard the monk inside speaking. He thought that the elder was reading from the Scripture. As he stood listening, he felt that the elder had gone mad through vainglory, and was ordaining himself a Deacon, and was dismissing the catechumens. When the visiting monk heard these things, he pushed the door and entered. The monk inside offered the customary greetings and wanted to learn if he had stood at the door a long time. The visiting elder said, amiably: "I came just now, when you recited the Dismissal (Ἀπόλυσις) of the catechumens." When the brother heard this, he fell to the feet of the elder and entreated him to pray for him, that he be delivered from this delusion.

I have recalled this in order to show to what insensibility this demon leads men. He who wants to contend perfectly and receive the crown of righteousness must strive by all means to defeat this multiform wild beast. He must always have in mind David's saying: "God scattered the bones of the men-pleasers."[60] Let him do nothing looking around for the praise of men. Let him seek only the reward of God. And ever discarding thoughts that come to his heart praising him, let him set himself at naught before God. In this way he will be able, with God's help, to free himself from the spirit of vainglory.

8. ON PRIDE

Our eighth struggle is against the spirit of pride (ὑπερηφάνεια). This struggle is the most difficult of all and the most fierce. It especially wages war against the perfect, and attempts to destroy those who have almost risen to the height of the virtues. And just as a pestilential and destructive disease does not damage one part of the body, but the whole body, so also pride, does not damage only some part of the soul, but the whole soul. In the case of the other passions,

[60] *Psalm* 52:6.

although each one disturbs the soul, it does so with reference to the virtue that is opposed to it, and strives to overcome it, and darkens the soul and disturbs it partially; but the passion of pride darkens the whole soul and brings it down to the terminal fall.

In order to apprehend more clearly what has been said, let us look at the matter in this way. Gluttony strives to corrupt self-restraint; fornication, temperance; avarice, non-possession of property; anger, meekness; and the rest of the passions, the other opposed virtues. The vice of pride, on the other hand, when it dominates the wretched soul, like a hard tyrant, having taken over a great and glorious city, destroys all of it and razes it down to the foundations. This is testified to by that Angel who fell down from Heaven through pride. He had been created by God and had been greatly adorned with every virtue. But he did not want to attribute this to the Lord's grace. Instead, he attributed it to himself. Accordingly, he considered himself to be equal to God. Censuring this thought, the Prophet said: "Thou didst say in thy heart: 'I shall sit on a high mountain. I shall set my throne upon the clouds, and shall be like the Highest,' but thou art not God."[61] And another Prophet says: "Why boastest thou, thyself in mischief?" And what

[61] Cf. *Isaiah* 14:13.

follows in the Psalm.[62]

Knowing these things, let us be afraid and guard our heart with greatest care, protecting it from the death-bringing spirit of pride, ever remembering the saying of the Apostle when we acquire some virtue: "Not I, but the grace of God which was with me."[63] Also, let us remember the saying of our Lord: "Without Me ye can do nothing,"[64] and that of the Prophet: "Except the Lord build the house, they labor in vain that build it,"[65] as well as that of the Apostle: "It is not of him that willeth nor of him that runneth, but of God that sheweth mercy."[66]

For even if one be very fervent in eagerness and seriousness in resolve, being conjoined with flesh and blood, he cannot attain perfection, except with the mercy of Christ and His grace. As James, too, says: "Every good gift and every perfect gift is from Above."[67] And as the Apostle Paul says: "What hast thou that thou didst not receive? Now if thou didst receive it, why dost thou glory, as if thou hast not received it?"[68]

[62] *Psalm* 51:1 ff.
[63] *1 Corinthians* 15:10.
[64] *John* 15:5.
[65] *Psalm* 126:1.
[66] *Romans* 9:16.
[67] *James* 1:17.
[68] *1 Corinthians* 4:7.

That it is by the grace and mercy of God that our salvation is effected is truthfully testified to by the thief, who did not win the prize of the Kingdom of Heaven through his virtue, but by the grace and mercy of God. All our Fathers, thoroughly knowing these things, handed down to us one and the same view, that one cannot attain perfection in virtue except through humility. This by nature is acquired through faith and fear of God, meekness, and perfect holy poverty. Through these, perfect love, too, is acquired. Through the grace and benevolence of our Lord Jesus Christ, to Whom glory forever. Amen.

BY THE SAME SAINT CASSIAN
TO ABBOT LEONTIOS
REGARDING THE HOLY FATHERS OF SKETE,
AND A VERY EDIFYING DISCOURSE
ON DISCERNMENT

Most holy Leontios, I have fulfilled part of my promise to the Most Blessed Archbishop Kastor regarding the account of the life of the holy Fathers and their teaching, and regarding the formation of the Coenobia, and the Eight Evil Thoughts. Now I undertake to pay my debt in full.

In view of the fact that I have learned that the Hierarch whom I mentioned has left us and departed to Christ, I judged it necessary to write to you the remainder of the story, inasmuch as you have succeeded him in virtue and, with the help of God, in the care of the monastery.

I went to the desert of Skete, where the most successful and noteworthy Fathers dwelt. Together with me was holy Germanos, who from the time of our childhood became my spiritual friend at the school, at the army, and in the monastic life. There we saw Abba Moses—a holy man who shone among the

219

others, not only in the practical virtues, but also in spiritual contemplation (πνευματικὴ θεωρία).

With tears we entreated him to tell us something edifying that would help us to attain perfection. After greatly entreating him he said to us: "My children, all the virtues and deeds have a certain aim, and those who have regard to that aim organize themselves and achieve their desired aim.

"Consider the farmer. He endures both heat and cold, and with eagerness cultivates the soil. He removes the thorns and weeds, and has as his aim to enjoy the fruits. Similarly, the merchant ignores the dangers, both of the sea and of the land, and proceeds in his business, having as his aim the profit from this activity, and his ultimate goal, the enjoyment of the profit. Again, he who enlists in the army, reckons neither the dangers of war, not the hardships in foreign lands, but has as his aim the acquisition of offices in recognition of his bravery and his goal the gain that results from his office.

"Now our endeavor, too, has its own particular aim and goal, for the sake of which we endure with eagerness all efforts and hardships. For this reason, abstinence from foods during the fasts does not knock us down. The effort of vigils pleases us. The reading of the Scriptures and meditation on their teachings is done with eagerness. The effort of our special tasks, obedience, and the renunciation of all earthly things, and dwelling in the desert, are things done gladly. You, who have disdained your father, your family, and the whole world, and have gone to a foreign land, and have come to me, who am a peasant and an ignorant man, tell me, what is your aim (σκοπός)? And to what goal (τέλος) is your aspiration directed?"

We replied: "To the Kingdom of Heaven."

To this, Abba Moses answered: "You replied well concerning your goal. However, you did not tell me what is the aim, looking at which, without deviating from the straight path, we may succeed in attaining to the Kingdom of Heaven."

Then, having confessed that we did not know, the Elder said: "So the goal of our monastic life, as you said, is the Kingdom of God. And the aim is the purity of the soul, without which it is impossible for us to attain to that goal. Therefore, our mind must always be directed to that aim. And if it ever happens that our heart deviates for a short while from the straight path, immediately we must bring it back to the aim, as by means of a builder's level.

"Knowing this, blessed Apostle Paul says: 'Forget–ting those things which are behind, I press forward towards the mark for the prize of the high calling of God.'[1] For this aim, therefore, we do everything, for this aim we despise everything: fatherland, family, money, and the whole world, in order to acquire purity of the heart. If we forget this aim, necessarily we walk in the dark. Outside the straight path we shall often stumble and will go far astray. This has happened to many, who at the beginning of their renunciation despised wealth, and money, and the whole world, but later on for the sake of a two-pointed mattock, or a needle, or a cane, or a book, got angry. This is something which would not have happened if they had remembered the aim for which they had despised everything. For the sake of love of our neighbor we despise wealth, so that we will not quarrel for it. By augmenting the disposition towards anger we fall from love. When for trivial things we reveal to our brother the disposition of anger, we have fallen from our aim and we have no benefit from our renunciation. As the Apostle Paul says: 'Though I give my body to be burned, and have not love, it profiteth me nothing.'[2]

"From this we learn that perfection does not come immediately following the renunciation of the

[1] *Philippians* 3:13-14.
[2] *1 Corinthians* 13:3.

world, but when we have achieved love, whose characteristics are described by the same Apostle, when he says: 'Love envieth not; love vaunteth not itself, is not puffed up by pride, is not easily provoked, thinketh no evil; rejoiceth not in iniquity.'[3] All these constitute the purity of the heart. For this we ought to do everything: despise money, gladly endure fasts and vigils, occupy ourselves with readings and psalms. And we must not neglect it, if some activity that is necessary and according to God should prevent you from the customary fasting and reading. For the benefit derived from fasting is not as great as the harm of anger. Neither is the benefit derived from reading as great as is the harm that results from the despising of our brother and grieving him.

"For as we said, fasting, vigils, the study of the Scriptures, and the stripping oneself of wealth, and the renunciation of the world do not constitute perfection (τελειότης), but are only instruments (ἐργαλεῖα) conducive to perfection. For perfection does not consist in these. They are only means to them. In vain, therefore, do we boast of fasting, vigil, non-possession of property, and reading the Scriptures, when we have not achieved love towards God and towards neighbor. For he who has achieved

[3] *Ibid.*, 13:4-6.

love has within himself God, and his mind is always with God."

To this, Germanos replied: "And who, united with the flesh, can have his mind always directed to God, having nothing in else in his mind? Neither visits to the sick, nor hospitality to strangers, nor handiwork, nor the needs of the body? And more importantly, how can the mind of man constantly see God, Who is invisible and incomprehensible, and to be inseparable from Him?"

Abba Moses replied: "For one to see God and to be inseparable from Him, in the way in which you think, is impossible for a man who is clothed with flesh and united with weakness. However, it is possible for one to see God in another way. For the contemplation of God takes place in many ways. God is not known according to His incomprehensible essence; this experience is reserved for the future life and only for His saints. But He is known through the magnificence and beauty (καλλονή) of His creatures, and from His daily government and providence, as well as from His justice and His miracles which He manifests to His saints. Therefore, when we think of His infinite power, His ever vigilant eye, which sees the secrets of the heart, and that nothing can escape His attention, then we experience awe in our heart, and we admire Him and worship Him. When we reflect that 'the drops of rain are numbered by Him,'[4] as are the grains of the sand in the sea and the stars in the firmament, we feel astonishment by the magnificence of nature and the wisdom exhibited by it. When we reflect on the ineffable and indescribable wisdom and loving-kindness of God and His incomprehensible forbearance which bears the innumerable faults of those who sin, we glorify Him. And when we reflect on His great love for us, that although we have done nothing good, He did not consider it unworthy of Him, although He is God, to become for us man, in order to save us from error, we are moved to long for him. When we reflect that He defeats within us our opponent, the devil,[5] and does so simply in response to our good deliberate choice and inclination towards the good, and grants to us eternal life, then we worship Him. And there are countless other comparable states of the mind that are engendered in us according to our spiritual life and purity, and by which God is manifested and known."

Germanos also asked: "What is the source of the following: Often, without our wishing, we are both-

[4] *Job* 36:27
[5] *1 Peter* 5:8

ered by many recollections and evil thoughts. And without our realizing it, they deceive us, entering secretly and noiselessly into our mind, so that not only are we unable to hinder them from coming, but also we have great difficulty to discern them with precision. We want to know if it is possible for our mind to remain altogether free from these thoughts, and not to be bothered at all by them."

To this, Abba Moses replied: "It is impossible for the mind not to be bothered by these thoughts. However, to receive them and either to examine them or to reject them is possible for a person who makes the effort. Their arising within us is not caused by us; but it is within our power to banish them. And the correction of our mind depends upon our deliberate choice and diligent effort. For when we continually meditate on the Law of God, and occupy ourselves with psalms and hymns, fasts and vigils, and remember continually the future life, the Kingdom of Heaven, the Hell of fire, and all the works of God, evil thoughts become fewer and find no place. When, however, we occupy ourselves with worldly cares and carnal things, and surrender ourselves to vain and unprofitable associations, then evil thoughts increase in number within us. Just as a watermill cannot stop so long as the water runs, and the miller is using it to grind wheat or weeds, similarly, our mind, being ever active, cannot remain idle, devoid of thoughts. And it is in our power to give it either spiritual meditation or carnal activity."

Abba Moses, seeing that we experienced admiration and astonishment with regard to all that he had said, and that we had insatiable desire for his words, after remaining silent for a while, said to us:

"Since your desire has occasioned the prolongation of my reply, and you are still eager to hear, I understand that you have a true thirst to hear a discussion on perfection. Therefore, I shall speak about the great virtue of discernment (διάκρισις). This is the acropolis and queen among the other virtues. And I shall show the superiority of this virtue, its sublimity and its benefits, not only by means of my own words, but also through the opinions of the holy Fathers, according to the Grace which the Lord grants—according to the worthiness and longing of the listeners—to those who explain His teaching.

"This virtue which is not small, but is one of the most outstanding gifts of the Holy Spirit, as the Apostle says: 'To one is given by the Spirit the word of wisdom; to another, the word of knowledge by the same Spirit; to another, faith by the same Spirit; to another, the gifts of healing by the same Spirit; to

another, discerning of spirits.'[6] After completing the
list of spiritual gifts, he says: 'All these worketh that
one and selfsame Spirit.' So you see that the gift of
discernment is not a small, or earthly gift, but a great
gift of Divine Grace. If a monk does not follow discernment with all his strength and eagerness, and
has not acquired sure discernment of the thoughts
that come to his mind, necessarily, like one wandering about during the night, not only will he fall into
the worst abysses of wickedness, but will also stumble on smooth and even places.

"I recall that once, when I was young, I went to
the regions of Thebaid, where blessed Antony had
dwelt. Some Elders had gathered about him and
they were discussing the perfection of virtue. Their
discussion focused on the question of which of the
virtues should be considered as the greatest one that
can protect a monk from the snares of the devil and
his deception, and unharmed. Each one reflected and
expressed his opinion. Some said that it was fasting
and vigil, because these virtues render the mind
subtle and render one pure, and thus more capable
of easily approaching God. Others said that it was
the total non-possession of property (ἀκτυμοσύνη)
and despising the things which one has, because

----

[6] *1 Corinthians* 12:8-10.

the mind is liberated from the complicated bonds of worldly cares, and can more easily come close to God. Others singled out the virtue of almsgiving, because the Lord says in the Gospel: 'Come, ye blessed of my Father, inherit the Kingdom prepared for you from the foundation of the world; for I was hungry, and ye gave me food' and so on.[7] And others singled out in this manner other virtues whereby, according to their opinion, man could approach God. And the greater part of the night passed in this way.

"The last one to speak on this subject was blessed Antony. He said: 'All these things which have been said are necessary and valuable for those who are seeking God and desire to come to Him. However, we should not give primacy to these virtues, for we have seen many who practiced great fasts and vigils, and withdrew to the desert, and were completely free from possessions, so that they did not even keep for themselves food for the next day, and practiced almsgiving to the point that they had given to others all that they had. Yet, later they fell from virtue in a deplorable way, and slid to badness. What was it that caused them to go astray from the straight path? Nothing else, in my judgment, but the fact that they

---

[7] *Matthew* 25:34-35.

did not have the gift of discernment. For discernment teaches man to avoid extremes of both kinds (excess and deficiency), and to walk on the royal path (of moderation). This path permits neither extreme self-restraint, whereby one is led astray on the right side, nor one's being drawn to indifference and slackness on the left side.

'Discernment is an eye of the soul, according to the Gospel, which says: 'The light of the body is the eye; if therefore thine eye be single, thy whole body shall be full of light. But if thine eye be evil, thy whole body shall be full of darkness.'[8] It is just so, because discernment both distinguishes everything that is evil and not pleasing to God, and distances one from error (πλάνη). One can learn this from what is narrated in the Holy Scriptures. Thus Saul, who was the first one to whom God entrusted the kingdom of Israel,[9] lacked this eye of discernment, and as a result his mind was darkened. He could not discern that it was more pleasing to God to obey the order of Samuel, than to offer a sacrifice. He erred by that which he thought, and was banished from the kingdom. This would not have happened to him if he had the light of discernment within himself.

[8] *Matthew* 6:22-23.
[9] *1 Kings* 13:8-14.

The Apostle calls this virtue sun, saying: "Let not the sun go down upon your wrath.'[10] It is also called the governor of our life, in accordance with the saying: 'They that have no guidance fall like leaves.'[11] It is also called in Scripture careful thought. And we are by Scripture to do nothing without discernment. The spiritual wine which gladdens the heart of man must not be drunk without discernment,[12] according to the saying: 'Drink wine attentively,'[13] and 'A city whose walls are broken down, and which is unfortified, so is a man who does anything without counsel.'[14] Wisdom, cognition, and inner perception involve discernment, and without these our inner house cannot be built. Neither can inner wealth be gathered, according to the saying: 'A house is built by wisdom, and is set up by understanding. By discernment the chambers are filled with all precious and excellent wealth.'[15] Discernment is also called the solid food of those who through askesis and habituation have their spiritual sense-organs trained and can easily distinguish between good and evil.'[16]

[10] *Ephesians* 4:26.
[11] *Proverbs* 11:14.
[12] *Psalm* 103:15.
[13] *Proverbs* 24:33.
[14] *Proverbs* 25:28.
[15] *Proverbs* 24:3-4.
[16] *Hebrews* 5:14.

"From these statements it is clearly proved that without the gift of discernment virtue is not formed, or does not remain firm until the end, discernment being the mother and guard of all the other virtues.

"This was the opinion of Antony. And all the other Fathers agreed with it. In order now to confirm the opinion of Saint Antony with contemporary examples, recall Father Heron and the pitiful event which took place a short time ago before our eyes. Recall in what manner, through the mockery of the devil, he fell from the height of spiritual life and askesis to the depth of death. We recall that for fifty years he dwelt at the nearby desert with great hardships and continuous self-restraint, and that he dwelt at the remotest desert and in greater solitude than all those here. After so many efforts and struggles he was mocked by the devil and fell to a very serious error, and plunged into the deepest, inconsolable sorrow, all the Fathers and Brethren who dwelt at the near desert. This would not have happened to him if he had been secured by the virtue of discernment. Discernment would have taught him not to trust his own thoughts, but the counsel of the Fathers and Brethren. Following his own thoughts, he practiced fasting and the avoidance of men, to such an extreme, that even during the feast of the Pascha he did not go to the church, lest he be invited by the Fathers and Brothers to eat pulses or something else that would be offered at the refectory, and he would think that he had abandoned the aim which he had set in his mind.

"Having gone astray during a long period of time by his own volitions, he received an angel of Satan. And having venerated him as an angel of light, he was ordered by him to fall into a very deep well at midnight, in order to learn that henceforth he will never be in danger, because of his great virtues and his godly efforts. Without reflecting with his mind who was giving him these counsels, in a state of mental darkness, he threw himself at midnight into the well. After a while the brothers learned about this, and with great effort succeeded in getting him out of the well half-dead. He lived for two days, and on the third day he died. He left Presbyter Paphnoutios and the brothers in a state of inconsolable mourning. Paphnoutios, moved by his great loving-kindness, and by his memory of his great ascetic struggles, and the many years during which he dwelt at the desert, did not reckon him among those who commit suicide, but performed for him the customary memorial services.

"What should I say about the two brothers who

dwelt beyond the Thebaid Desert, where blessed Antony once dwelt? These two, incited by a thought devoid of discernment, decided to go to the remoter desert, which is great and uncultivated, and there not to receive food from a man, but only what God would give them through some miracle. They were seen by the Mazikes, wandering in the desert, exhausted by starvation.

"Although both brothers reflected wrongly from the beginning, and made a rash and destructive decision, one of them, because discerning had emerged in him, corrected his insolent and foolish decision. The other, by abiding in his foolish idea, remained devoid of discernment and provoked his own death.

"What shall I say about him, whose name I do not wish to mention, because he dwells in this vicinity? He often welcomed a demon as an angel, and received revelations from him, and saw continuously the light of a lantern inside his cell. Finally, he was ordered by the demon to sacrifice his son, who dwelt together with him at his hermitage, as a sacrifice to God, and thus to receive the honor of the Patriarch Abraham. He assented completely to the demon's advice and would have slain his son, had not his son noticed his father sharpening his knife and readying ropes in order to bind him tightly as a holocaust, and had he not hastened to run away to safety.

"I would extend my account very much, if I should narrate to you in detail the deception of a monk from Mesopotamia, who exhibited great self-restraint, and remained during many years confined to his cell, and then was made a fool and was deceived by the devil through demonic revelations and dreams—after so many efforts and virtues, by which he had surpassed all the other monks there. He fell to Judaism and accepted circumcision. For the devil, wishing to deceive him, often showed him true dreams, in order thereby to dispose him to easily accept the deception to which he would finally lead him. Thus, one night he showed him all the Christians, together with the Apostles and the Martyrs, in a state of darkness and full of every sort of shame and dishonor, and in a state of sorrow and mourning. And on the other hand, he showed the Hebrews, together with Moses and the other Prophets, illuminated by bright light and full of joy and gladness. The deceiver advised the monk that if he wanted to enjoy the blessedness and joy of the Hebrews he should accept circumcision. And the monk actually was deceived and did that.

"It is manifest from what I have said, that all the monks that I have described would not have become playthings, in such a wretched and pitiful manner, if they had the gift of discernment."

To these accounts, Germanos added the following: "From the examples and explanations of the early Fathers, it has been sufficiently proved that discernment is the fount and root and binding together of all the virtues. However, we wish to learn how we can acquire discernment, and how we can distinguish godly discernment from pseudo discernment, which is of diabolic nature."

Then Abba Moses said: "True discernment is not acquired otherwise than by true humility, by revealing to Spiritual Fathers, not only what we do, but also our thoughts, and by our not trusting our thoughts in anything, but following in all things the teachings of the Elders, and regarding as good whatever they approve of.

"In this way, not only does a monk remain unharmed, having true discernment and the right standpoint, but also is kept safe from all the snares of the devil. It is impossible for one who orders his life in accord with the judgment and view of advanced Fathers to be deceived by the demons.

Before one is deemed worthy of the gift of discernment, the very revelation of one's evil thoughts to the Fathers withers and weakens such thoughts. Just as a serpent, when it gets out of its dark hole hastens in order to be saved, so also evil thoughts, when they are brought to light through true confession, hasten to depart from a man.

"In order that you might learn with greater precision and by means of examples about the virtue of discernment, I shall speak about something in the life of Abba Serapion, about which he spoke to those who went to him for their protection. He used to say: 'When I was younger, I dwelt with my Elder. When we ate and rose from the table, by the incitement of the devil I used to steal a biscuit (παξιμάδι) and eat it secretly. Having done this over a long period of time, I was overcome by this passion and could not overcome it. I was censured, however, by my conscience, but was ashamed to tell it to my Elder. Providentially, it chanced that some Brothers came to him for their personal benefit. The Elder said to them that nothing harms monks and causes joy to the demons so much as one's hiding one's thoughts from one's Spiritual Father. He also spoke about self-restraint. As he said these things, I came to myself and reflected that God had revealed my sins to my Elder, and I experienced compunction and started to weep. Then I took the biscuit which I had stolen and hidden in my bosom. It fell on the ground and I began asking for forgiveness for the biscuits which

I had stolen, and for prayers so that I might not do that again.

Then the Elder said: "My child, you have been freed without my speaking. By your confession and by your silence, you have slain the demon who has been wounding you—the demon who has been mastering you until now with your assent, for you neither opposed him nor censured him. Henceforth, he will have no place in your heart, since you have manifested him.

The Elder had not finished speaking, and the demonic energy came out of my breast like fire, and the house was filled with a foul odor, so that those present thought that sulfur was burning.

Then the Elder said: 'Behold, by this sign the Lord gave proof of my words and of your liberation.'

"Thus, through my confession there departed from me the passion of gluttony and that of diabolic influence, so that never again did there come to me an inclination for the desire.

"You see then, from the words of Abba Serapion, that we learn that we become worthy of the gift of true discernment when we do not put our trust in our own thoughts and judgments, but in the teaching and rules of our Fathers. For by means of no other fault does the devil lead a monk so much to the precipice as by persuading him to transgress the counsels of the Fathers and to follow his own opinions and volitions.

"We ought to take examples also from the secular arts and sciences (τὰς ἀνθρωπίνας τέχνας καὶ ἐπιστήμας), and learn from them. Here we need one who will teach us correctly their rules; and it is foolish to think that in the spiritual art, (τὴν πνευματικὴν τέχνην) which is the most difficult of the arts we do not need a teacher. This art is invisible, hidden, and is apprehended by one who has purity of the heart. Failure in this art results not just in transitory damage, but also in the perdition of the soul, in eternal death.

Germanos said: "It is a shame that some of the Fathers, after hearing the thoughts of their brothers, not only do not heal them, but reproach them and cast them into despair. We have had occasion to learn about one such event in Syria. A brother there confessed his thoughts to an Elder, with great simplicity and sincerity. He laid bare, and without shame, the secrets of his heart. As soon as the Elder heard these, he became disgusted and angry at his brother, blaming him for his evil thoughts. This event resulted, in the case of many who learned about it, in being afraid to confess their thoughts.

Abba Moses replied: "It is good, as I said earlier, not

to conceal our thoughts from the Fathers. However, not to tell them to chance persons, but to spiritual Elders who have discernment. Not to those who are merely very advanced in years. For many, paying regard only to the age, confessed their thoughts, and instead of finding therapy fell into despair, owing to the inexperience of the Elders. There was a brother who was very eager in askesis. He was annoyed very much by the demon of fornication, and went to an Elder and told him his thoughts. The Elder listened to him, and because he was inexperienced he was filled with disgust. He called the monk wretched and unworthy of the monastic habit, because he assented to such thoughts. When the brother heard this, he fell into despair, and left his place and took the road to return to the world. By divine dispensation, on the way, he met Abbot Apollos, the most experienced among the Elders. When he saw him troubled and sullen, he asked him: 'My child, what is the cause of your great sorrow?' At the beginning, owing to his great despair, the novice did not reply. Afterward, following the insistent entreaties of Apollos, he explained: 'I am troubled by many thoughts, and I went and told them to Elder so-and-so. He told me that I have no hope of salvation. So despairing, I am returning to the world.' When Father Apollos heard this, He told him many consoling words, and counseled him, saying: 'Let it not appear strange to you, and do not despair. I, too, at the age that I am, with white hair, am very much annoyed by these thoughts. Do not lose your courage by the heating of your body, which is not cured so much by human care as by the loving kindness of God. Just grant me this day and return to your cell. The brother did that. The Abbot, Apollos, too, left, and went to the cell of the Elder who had led the brother to despair. And having stood outside, he entreated God with tears saying: 'Thou Who doest send temptations for our benefit, turn the war, which the young brother went through, to this Elder, in order that he might learn now in his old age, experientially, what he did not learn during so many years, in order that he might learn to suffer with, and have sympathy for, those who are assaulted.' As soon as he finished his prayer he saw a black cloud standing near the cell and throwing arrows against the Elder, by which he was hit, and at once began going about as if drunk. Unable to endure inside his cell, he went outside, and headed for the world, on the same road that had been taken by the younger brother. Abba Apollos understood what had happened, and approached him and said to him: "Where are you going? And what is the cause of your agita-

tion? He perceived that the thing had been revealed
to the holy Abbot, but from shame he did not say
anything. And Abbot Apollos said to him: "Return
to your cell and henceforth be aware of your weakness. And believe that the devil either had forgotten
you, or despised you, that is why there was no occasion for you to wrestle with him. You were not able
to endure an assault of the devil, even for one day.
That which happened, happened because when you
received a young brother who was attacked by the
common enemy, instead of strengthening him in the
common struggle, you cast him into despair. For no
one could endure the assaults of the enemy, nor endure the boiling of nature which scalds, if the grace
of God did not protect human weakness.

"So, the dispensation of God for your salvation
having been completed, let us together entreat God
to withdraw the affliction which has come upon you.
For He causes us to experience pain, and He also
heals us.[17] He humbles us and elevates us. He morti-
fies us and gives us life, He lowers us to Hades and
raises us to Heaven.[18]

Having said these things, Abbot Apollos prayed
and at once freed him from the war of fornication,

[17] *Job* 5:10.
[18] *1 Kings* 2:6-7.

advised him to pray to God that he be given enlightened tongue, so that he might say the appropriate words when occasion arises.

"From all the things that we have said, we learn that there will not be found a safe path that leads to salvation other than that of confessing our thoughts to Fathers who have great discernment, and receiving from them instructions for virtue, and not to follow our own judgment and our thoughts. Even if someone happens to meet a simple Elder, or certain others who lack experience, one must not avoid revealing one's thoughts to very experienced Fathers, despising the tradition of our forefathers. For they, too, were not moved by their own will, but by God and the divinely inspired Scriptures, and handed this to later Fathers—that is to receive counsel from those who are advanced in virtue. This we can learn from many passages in Holy Scripture, especially from the story of Samuel. Although from childhood he had been dedicated by his mother to God, and was deemed worthy of conversing with God, he did not trust his own thought, but once and twice hastened to his Elder Elei and received instructions from him, as to how to respond to God.[19] And he whom God has selected as worthy of Him, wants to be guided

[19] *1 Kings* 3:9.

by the counsel and command of his Elder, in order to
be led to humility. And Paul, whom Christ Himself
called, and talked with him, could immediately open
his eyes and show him the path of perfection, sends
him to Ananias, and commands him to learn from
Ananias the path of truth, saying: "Arise, and go into
the city, and it shall be told what thou must do."[20] In
this way He teaches us to follow the guidance of those
who have progressed. This shows that we should be
led to the truth through the Fathers. That things are
so we can learn not only from what we have already
said, but also from other things that Paul showed
in his life. Thus, he wrote: "I went up to Jerusalem
to meet Peter and James, to announce to them the
Gospel which I preached, lest I am running and have
run in vain." Yet, he was accompanied by the grace
of the Holy Spirit, as is evident from the power of the
miracles which he performed. Who then is so arrogant and proud as to follow his own opinion, when
the 'vessel of selection' confesses that he needed the
counsel of the older ones of the Apostles?

"These things manifestly prove that to no one does
the Lord reveal the path to perfection, except to those
who are guided by Spiritual Fathers. As He says
through the mouth of the Prophet: 'Ask your Father

[20] *Acts of the Apostles* 9:6.

and he will tell you, ask those who are advanced in years and they will respond.'[21]

Therefore, with all our strength and care we must acquire within us the precious gift of discernment, which will preserve us unharmed from every excess. For as the Fathers say, the extremes of both sides (excess and deficiency) do harm: both extreme fasting and satiety of the belly, both excessive vigil and satiety of sleep, as well as the other forms of too much and too little. We know some who were not defeated by gluttony but were defeated by extreme fasting, their health having been undermined, they fell to the passion of gluttony, owing to the weakness that resulted from their extreme fasting. I remember that I myself suffered such a thing. Again, assenting to the suggestion of the devil, to practice excessive vigil, I ended up with insomnia, and for many nights I remained sleepless, and entreated the Lord to give me a little sleep. Thus, I was endangered more by excessive fasting and sleeplessness than by gluttony and satiety of sleep."

By such and so many teachings holy Moses delighted us, and benefited us. And we gloried the Lord, Who grants such great wisdom to those who fear Him. To Him belong honor and power unto the ages. Amen.

[21] *Deuteronomy* 32:7.

SAINT MARK THE ASCETIC

CHAPTER 5

BRIEF BIOGRAPHY OF OUR HOLY AND GOD-BEARING FATHER MARK THE ASCETIC

Whose memory is celebrated on March 5

Our holy Father Mark the Ascetic flourished about the year 430. He was a disciple of Saint John Chrysostom, according to Nikephoros Kallistos (Vol. 2, Book 14, Chapter 53), and a contemporary of Saints Neilos and Isidoros of Pelusion, famous ascetics. Being industrious and having devoted himself to the study of the Holy Scriptures, he wrote many discourses full of every kind of instruction and profit.

Thirty-two of his discourses are mentioned by Nikephoros Kallistos as teaching the entire ascetic way of life. But they are not to be found now. There survive only eight of his discourses, different from these. Kallistos himself and the discerning Photios (*Reading* 200, p. 268) mention these eight discourses.

The first discourse is *Concerning Spiritual Law*; the second is *On Those Who Think that One is Justified by Works*. Both are divided into brief chapters that are easily taken in at a glance. The third is addressed *To the Monk Nicholaos*. These three discourses have been selected for inclusion here, as being more useful than the others and having reference to spiritual law.

The writings of Saint Mark are mentioned by the Hosiomartyr Peter Damascene, Saint Gregory (Palamas) of Thessaloniki, Saint Gregory the Sinaite, the most holy Patriarch Kallistos, Pavlos Evergetinos, and many other Fathers. Having read these works, they exhort us also to read them.

The Holy Church of Christ, honoring Saint Mark, commemorates him on the 5th of March, and proclaims his ascetic struggles, the wisdom contained in his discourses, and the gift of miracles which was granted to him from Above.

200 TEXTS CONCERNING SPIRITUAL LAW BY OUR HOLY AND GOD-INSPIRED FATHER MARK THE ASCETIC

1. Because you have often wished to know how the Law (Νόμος) is spiritual, according to the Apostle, and what is the knowledge (γνῶσις) and the work (ἐργασία) of those who wish to keep it, we shall speak of it as far as we are able.

2. Firstly, we know that God is the beginning, middle, and end of every good. But it is inconceivable for the good to be the object of action or to be believed in except in Christ Jesus and the Holy Spirit.

3. Every good (ἀγαθόν) is given by the Lord providentially; and he who believes thus will not lose it.

4. Steadfast faith is a mighty tower. And Christ becomes everything for him who believes.

5. Let the governor of all good govern every plan of yours, in order that the project might be achieved according to God.

6. He who is humble and engages in spiritual work, when reading the Divine Scriptures will take everything to apply to himself and not to someone else.

7. Invoke God to open the eyes of your heart so that you might see the profitableness of prayer and of reading, which is understood through experience.

8. He who has some spiritual gift and feels sympathy for those who do not have it, through the sympathy preserves the gift. But the arrogant man will lose it, being overcome by arrogant thoughts.

9. The mouth of a humble man (ὁ ταπεινόφρων) speaks truth; whereas he who speaks against it is like the servant who struck the Lord on the jaw with the palm of his hand (*John* 18:22).

10. Do not become a disciple of one who praises himself, lest you learn pride instead of humility.

11. Do not exalt yourself in your heart regarding certain ideas contained in Scripture, lest you fall mentally to the spirit of blasphemy.

12. Do not attempt to explain something difficult by disputation, but through the means which spiritual law indicates: through patience and prayer and unwavering hope.

13. He is blind, crying and saying: "Son of David, have mercy on me" (*Luke* 18:38), who prays physically and does not yet possess spiritual knowledge.

14. When the man who at one time was blind received his sight and saw the Lord, he no longer confessed that He was the Son of David, but the Son of

God, and worshipped Him (*John* 9:38).

15. Do not exalt yourself when you shed tears in your prayer, for Christ has touched your eyes and you have received spiritual sight.

16. He who, in imitation of the blind man, casts away his garment and approaches the Lord, becomes His follower and a preacher of the most perfect doctrines.

17. Vice, when meditated on, emboldens the heart; but when it is destroyed by self-restraint and hope, the heart becomes contrite.

18. There is crushing of the heart which is equable and conducive to its contrition, and there is another which is uneven and harmful, as a rebuke of it.

19. Vigil (ἀγρυπνία), prayer and patient endurance of what befalls one constitute a crushing that is free from harm and helpful for the heart; only if we do not destroy their commixture through greed. He who perseveres in these will also be helped in the rest. Whereas he who is negligent and languid will suffer intolerably in his departure from this life.

20. A pleasure-loving heart becomes a prison and chain for the soul at the time of departure; whereas a painstaking one is an open door.

21. "The iron gate that leadeth unto the city" (*Acts* 12:10) is a hard heart. The gate will open of its

own accord to him who suffers and is afflicted, as to Peter." (*Acts* 12:10).

22. There are many methods of prayer, one more different than another. But not one method of prayer is harmful, except if it is not prayer but a satanic activity.

23. A man who wished to do evil first prayed in mind according to his habit, and having been providentially hindered, he afterwards gave many thanks.

24. When David wanted to kill Nabal the Carmelite, he received a reminder of divine retribution and abandoned his proposed end, and gave many thanks" (*1 Kings* ch. 25). Again, we know what he did when he forgot God, and did not cease, until Nathan the Prophet led him to memory of God (*1 Kings* ch. 14).

25. At the time when you remember God, increase your prayer, in order that when you forget, God may remind you.

26. When you read the Divine Scriptures, reflect on the things hidden in them. "For whatsoever things were written aforetime were written for our learning." (*Romans* 15:4).

27. Scripture speaks of faith as "the substance of things hoped for" (*Hebrews* 11:1), and calls repro-

bates those who do not know the indwelling of Jesus (*2 Corinthians* 13:5).

28. Just as a thought becomes manifest through deeds and words, so does the future recompense become manifest through the benefactions of the heart.

29. Thus, a merciful heart will obtain mercy; while about the opposite nature sequence gives the answer.

30. The law of freedom teaches every truth. Many read this according to their knowledge, but few understand it, each in proportion to his fulfilling of the Commandments.

31. Do not seek the perfection of the fulfilling of the Commandments in human virtues, for it is not found perfect in them. Its perfection is hidden in the Cross of Christ.

32. The law of freedom is read through true knowledge, is understood through the fulfilling of the Commandments, and is completed through the mercies of Christ.

33. When through conscience we are forced to carry out all the Commandments of God, then we shall understand that the law of the Lord is perfect (*Psalm* 18:8 – Septuagint); that it is put into practice in our fair deeds, but cannot find perfect fulfillment in hu-

man actions without the mercies of God.

34. Those who have not reckoned themselves debtors of every Commandment of Christ read the law of God in a non-spiritual manner, "understanding neither what they say nor whereof they affirm" (*1 Timothy* 1:7). Therefore they think that they fulfill it by their deeds.

35. There are things done which seem good, but the purpose of him who does them is not good; and there are other things which seem bad, while the purpose of their doer is good. Some not only perform deeds, but also make statements in the manner which we have just mentioned. Of these, some exchange things because of inexperience or ignorance; others, because of evil intention; and still others through pious aim.

36. He who offers praises while harboring slander and blame is hard to find out for simpler people. Similar to him is the man who is vainglorious but pretends to be humble. These men misrepresent the truth for a long time. Later they are exposed by things and are rebuked.

37. There is a man who does something that seems plainly to be good, defending his neighbor; and there is a man who, by not doing it, has benefited in the mind.

38. There is reproof in accordance with wickedness and self-defense; and there is another reproof, which is in accordance with God and truth.

39. No longer reprove him who has ceased from sin and has finally repented. If you say that you reprove him according to God, first expose your own evils.

40. God is the source of every virtue, as the sun is of daylight.

41. Having done a virtuous act, remember Him who says that "without me ye can do nothing" (*John* 15:5).

42. Goods are prepared for men through tribulation (cf. *Acts of the Apostles* 14:22); similarly, evils are prepared through vainglory and pleasure.

43. He who suffers injustice from men escapes sin, and finds help which is a match for the tribulation.

44. He who believes in Christ concerning retribution readily endures every injustice, in proportion to his faith.

45. He who prays for men who wrong him dashes down demons; whereas he who sets himself against the former is wounded by the latter.

46. Better an offence of men than one of demons. He who pleases the Lord has vanquished both.

47. Every good from God comes providentially.

But this fact mysteriously escapes the notice of the ungrateful, the senseless, and the idle.

48. Every vice ends up in forbidden pleasure; and every virtue, in spiritual consolation. When the former prevails, it stimulates what is related to it; and when the latter, similarly it stimulates what is akin to it.

49. Censure from men causes tribulation to the heart, but to him who patiently endures it, becomes a cause of purity.

50. Ignorance (ἄγνοια) disposes one to speak in opposition to what is profitable; and when it becomes bold, it increases the consequences of vice.

51. Suffering no loss, accept afflictions; and since you will give an account (cf. *Hebrews* 13:17), cast away greed.

52. Having sinned secretly, do not attempt to escape notice. For "all things are naked and opened unto the eyes" of the Lord (*Hebrews* 4:13), to whom we are accountable.

53. Show yourself mentally to the Master. "For man looketh on the outward appearance, but the Lord looketh on the heart" (*1 Samuel* 16:7).

54. Consider nothing and do nothing without a purpose which is according to God. For he who journeys aimlessly will labor in vain.

55. For him who sins without constraint, sin becomes hard to be repented, because nothing can escape the notice of God's justice.

56. A painful happening brings memory of God to a man who possesses understanding; it correspondingly saddens the man who forgets God.

57. Let every involuntary pain become a teacher of memory (of God), and you will not lack occasions for repentance.

58. Forgetfulness (λήθη) as such has no power, but gains strength from our own negligence (ἀμέλεια) and in proportion to it.

59. Do not say, "What can I do?" For I do not want it, and it comes; because in remembering, you reasoned falsely about your duty.

60. Do the good which you remember; and that which you do not remember will be revealed to you. And do not give up your thought to indiscriminate forgetfulness.

61. Scripture says: "Hell and perdition are manifest to the Lord" (*Proverbs* 15:11 – Septuagint). It says this about ignorance and forgetfulness of the heart.

62. For hell is ignorance, both being obscure. And perdition is forgetfulness, for they (memories) perished from a state of existence.[1]

[1] The meaning of the text here is obscure.

63. Investigate your own evils and not those of your neighbor; and your spiritual workshop (τὸ νοηρὸν ἐργαστήριον) will not be taken away.

64. Negligence with regard to all the goods that are within our power is difficult to forgive. But mercy and prayer rally (ἀνακαλεῖται) those who have been negligent.

65. All suffering (θλίψις) according to God is a substantial result of piety; for true love is tested by adversities.

66. Do not say that you have acquired virtue without suffering; for virtue acquired without suffering (θλῖψις) is untried, because of ease.

67. Consider the outcome of every involuntary suffering, and you will find in it the destruction of sin.

68. Many are the counsels of one's neighbor regarding one's interest. But to each one nothing is more fitting than one's own opinion.

69. If you are seeking to be cured, give heed to your conscience, and do everything which it tells you, and you shall receive benefit.

70. The hidden things of each one are known by God and by conscience. Let one receive correction from them.

71. Man pursues whatever he can according to his own will; but God causes the outcome of these to be

in accordance with justice.

72. If you wish to receive praise from men without condemnation, first love reproof for your sins.

73. One shall be glorified by people a hundredfold for the humiliation which he receives for the sake of the truth of Christ. And it is better to do every good for the sake of future blessings.

74. When a man benefits another man by words or deeds, let both perceive the presence of God's grace. He who does not understand this will be held under authority by him who understands it.

75. One who praises his neighbor in accordance with a certain hypocrisy will in time revile him and will himself be disgraced.

76. He who ignores the ambush of the enemy is easily slain; and he who does not know the causes of the passions easily falls.

77. From love of pleasure comes negligence; and from negligence, forgetfulness. For God has given to all knowledge of the things that are to our interest.

78. A man advises his neighbor according to his own knowledge. But God works effectively in him who listens according to his faith.

79. I have seen unlearned men who became humble in deed; and they became wiser than the wise.

80. Other unlearned men, upon hearing themselves

praised, did not imitate their humility, but becoming vainglorious about being unlearned, fell into pride.

81. He who belittles understanding and boasts of ignorance is unlearned not only in word but also in knowledge (cf. *2 Corinthians* 11:6).

82. Just as wisdom of words is one thing and prudence another, so being unlearned in words is one thing and folly is another.

83. Ignorance of words will not harm at all a very devout person, nor will wisdom of words harm one who is humble.

84. Do not say: "I do not know what is right, therefore I am guiltless when I do not do it. For if you did all the good deeds which you know, the rest would subsequently be revealed to you, one being understood through the other, after the manner of small rooms. It is not to your interest before doing the former to know the latter. For "knowledge puffeth up," through idleness, "but love edifieth," because it "beareth all things" (*1 Corinthians* 8:1; 13:7).

85. Read the words of Divine Scripture through deeds, and do not babble, being puffed up by bare notions (ψιλὰ νοήματα).

86. He who neglects deeds and leans upon bare knowledge, holds instead of a double-edged sword a staff of reed, which in time of war, according to

Scripture, will go into his hand and pierce it (*2 Kings* 18:21), injecting the poison of nature prior to the enemy.

87. Every thought has its measure and standard (μέτρον καὶ σταθμόν) from God. For it is possible to consider the same thing either passionately or simply.

88. Let him who has fulfilled a commandment expect a temptation on behalf of it. For our love of Christ is tested by adversities.

89. Never think lightly of negligence of thoughts. For no thought can escape the detection of God.

90. When you see a thought which suggests to you human glory, realize clearly that it is preparing dishonor for you.

91. The enemy knows the justice of spiritual law and only seeks mental assent. Thus, he will either make the man who is under his power liable to the suffering of repentance or, if the man does not repent, he will cause him suffering through happenings against his will. Also, there are times when he disposes a man to resist the happenings in order that in this way, too, he might multiply the suffering, and at the time of departure prove the man faithless through lack of patient endurance.

92. Many men have set many things against the

events that befell them; but without prayer and repentance no one has escaped an evil.

93. Evils acquire their power through one another; similarly goods increase through each other; and they incite him who shares in them onwards with greater intensity.

94. The devil disparages small sins. For otherwise he is unable to lead us to greater evils.

95. The root of shameful desire is human praise, just as the root of chastity is the reproof of vice – when we not only hear the reproof, but also accept it.

96. He who has renounced the world yet leads a life of pleasure has derived no benefit at all. For what he used to do through possessions he now does having nothing.

97. Again, the self-restrained man, if he acquires money, is a brother, according to the mind, of the man just mentioned; for they have the same mother, through mental pleasure, though they have a different father through the change of the passion.

98. There is a man who cuts off a passion for the sake of greater pleasures, and he is praised by those who do not know his purpose. And perhaps he is ignorant of himself, since he does foolish things.

99. A cause of every vice is vainglory and pleasure; and he who has not come to hate them does not strip

off a passion.

100. "The love of money," it is said, "is the root of all evil" (*1 Timothy* 6:10); but this vice is clearly made up of vainglory and love of pleasure.

101. The mind is blinded by these three passions: love of money, vainglory, and pleasure.

102. These are the three daughters of the leech dearly loved by their mother folly, according to Scripture (*Proverbs* 30:15 – Septuagint).

103. Knowledge and faith, the companions of our nature, were blunted through nothing else but them.

104. Anger, wrath, wars, murders and all the rest of the list of evils have through them become strong among men.

105. Thus it is necessary to hate the love of money, vainglory, and pleasure, as mothers of evils and stepmothers of virtues.

106. On account of them we have been commanded not to love "the world" and "the things that are in the world" (*1 John* 2:15); not in order that we might hate indiscriminately the creatures of God, but in order that we might eliminate the occasions of those three passions.

107. "No one," says the Apostle, "that warreth entangleth himself with the affairs of this life" (2

Timothy 2:4). For he who wishes to overcome the passions after he has entangled himself with them is like a man who is extinguishing a conflagration by means of straw.

108. He who becomes angry with his neighbor on account of money, or glory, or pleasure does not yet know that God governs things with justice.

109. When you hear the Lord saying that "if someone forsaketh not all that he hath," he is not worthy of me (*Luke* 14:33), do not take this statement to refer only to money, but also to all the actions of vice.

110. He who does not know the truth cannot have true faith either. For knowledge according to nature precedes faith.

111. Just as God has distributed to each of the visible things what is fitted for it, so also to human thoughts, whether we want it or not.

112. If someone who manifestly sins, and does not repent, has suffered nothing until his departure, you may conclude that judgment in his case will be merciless.

113. He who prays wisely, patiently endures the events that befall him, whereas he who bears malice has not yet prayed purely.

114. If you have suffered a loss, or been reviled, or persecuted by someone, do not consider the present,

but wait for the future, and you will find that he has become for you a cause of many goods, not only in the present, but also in the life to come.

115. Just as bitter wormwood benefits those who have a poor appetite, so it is profitable for the malicious to suffer evils. For as medicines they promote the physical wellbeing of the former and dispose the latter to repent.

116. If you do not wish to suffer evil, then do not wish to do evil either, because the latter inviolably follows the former. "For whatever a man soweth, that shall he also reap" (*Galatians* 6:7).

117. Voluntarily sowing evil and involuntarily reaping it, we ought to admire the justice of God.

118. Because a period of time has been allotted between sowing and reaping, we disbelieve in retribution (or, according to other texts: we ought not to disbelieve in retribution).

119. Having sinned, do not allege the overt act as the cause, but the thought. For if the mind had not run in advance, the body would not have followed.

120. The secret evildoer is more wicked than those who do evil openly. Wherefore he receives more painful punishment.

121. He who weaves wiles and does evil secretly is a serpent, according to Scripture, "besetting the

road and biting the heel of the horse" (*Genesis* 39:17 – Septuagint).

122. He who at one time praises his neighbor to some man, and censures him to another, has been mastered by vainglory and envy. Through praise he attempts to hide his envy, and through censure to recommend himself as of better repute than his neighbor.

123. Just as it is not possible for sheep and wolves to feed at the same place (*The Wisdom of Jesus, the Son of Sirach*, 13:17), so it is impossible for a man who is treacherous to his neighbor to receive mercy.

124. He who secretly mixes his own will with an injunction is an adulterer, as it is shown in the *Wisdom* (*Proverbs* 6:32-33); and through lack of sense he endures pains and dishonor.

125. Just as water and fire oppose union, so self-justification and humility are opposed to one another.

126. He who seeks forgiveness of sins loves humility. But he who condemns another confirms his own evils.

127. Do not leave your sin unblotted out, even though it should happen to be extremely small, lest afterward it carry you away to greater evils.

128. If you wish to be saved, love words of truth, and never indiscriminately turn away from reproof.

129. Words of truth changed the "generation of vipers" and warned them "to flee from the wrath to come" (*Matthew* 3:7).

130. He who receives words of truth receives God the Logos; for He says: "He that receiveth you receiveth me" (*Matthew* 10:40).

131. A paralytic who is let down through the housetop is a sinner who is reproved by the faithful according to God and who receives forgiveness through their faith.

132. It is better to pray with piety for your neighbor than to reprove him for every sinful action.

133. He who repents rightly is derided by the foolish. This is a sign for him that he has pleased God.

134. He who is struggling spiritually always exercises self-restraint. And he does not cease struggling until the Lord destroys "seed out of Babylon" (*Jeremiah* 27:16 – Septuagint).

135. Reckon that the passions of disgrace are twelve. If you should love one of them, this will make up for the other eleven.

136. Sin is a burning fire. The more you diminish the matter, the more it will be quenched. And in proportion as you add to it, it will burn with greater intensity.

137. Having exalted yourself because of praise, accept dishonor. For He says: "Whosoever exalteth himself shall be abased" (*Luke* 14:11).

138. When we have put away every voluntary badness of the mind, then in turn we shall fight against the passions at the stage of predisposition (πρόληψις).

139. A predisposition is an involuntary remembrance of former evils. It is prevented by him who struggles against its developing into a passion; but it is overthrown by the victor when it has gone no further than the stage of suggestion (προσβολή).

140. Suggestion is a movement of the heart without images.

141. Where there are images of thoughts, there assent (συγκατάθεσις) has taken place. For guiltless suggestion is a movement without sinful images. There is a man who flees away from these "like a brand plucked out of fire" (*Zacharias* 3:2); and there is a man who does not retire until the fire lights up.

142. Do not say: "I do not want it," and yet it comes. For at any rate, if you do not love it, you love the causes of the thing.

143. He who seeks praise is involved in passion. And when affliction comes, he who laments bitterly desires pleasure.

144. The thought of the voluptuous man is unsettled, as on a balance; sometimes he weeps and laments bitterly for his sins, and sometimes he fights against and contradicts his neighbor, pursuing pleasures.

145. He who proves all things and holds fast that which is good (*1 Thessalonians* 5:21) will as a consequence escape every evil.

146. A patient man has much prudence (φρόνησις), similarly, he who turns his ear to words of wisdom.

147. Without remembrance of God, it is impossible for knowledge to be true. For without the former, the latter is counterfeit.

148. Words of subtler knowledge benefit the hard-hearted man, awakening fear. For without fear he does not accept the pains of repentance.

149. For a meek man frank speech is helpful, inasmuch he does not make trial of God's longsuffering and has not been wounded by frequent transgression.

150. Do not reprove a powerful man for his vainglory, but show him the penalty of the future dishonor. For in this manner an intelligent man is suavely reproved.

151. He who hates reproof (cf. *Proverbs* 12:1) is predisposed to passion. But he who loves reproof,

manifestly goes against the predisposition.

152. Have no desire to hear about the villainies of others. For through such a desire the character of the villainies are inscribed (in the soul).

153. Having become fond of evil words, be angry with yourself, not with others who use them. For when the things said are evil, he who utters them also will be evil.

154. If someone should fall in with men who talk idly, he should consider himself as responsible for such talk; if not on a recent occasion, on an older one.

155. If you see someone praising you hypocritically, at the same time expect censure from him.

156. Exchange present afflictions for future goods, and error will never weaken your struggle.

157. When, for the sake of an offering for a bodily need, you praise someone as good, not according to God, afterward the same man will manifest himself to you as evil.

158. Every good comes from the Lord providentially. And those who bring them are servants of good things.

159. Accept with an equable mind the alternation of goods and evils. It is thus that God checks the irregularity of things.

160. The inequality of thoughts brings about their own changes. For God has fittingly portioned out the involuntary to the voluntary.

161. Things perceptible by the senses spring from spiritual things, bringing what is needful by God's decree.

162. From a voluptuous heart arise pestilent thoughts and words; and from the smoke we recognize the matter involved.

163. Stand by the mind (διάνοια) and you will not be troubled by temptations. But if you depart from it, bear what befalls you.

164. Pray that temptation may not come to you (*Matthew* 6:13). When it comes, accept it as yours and not another's.

165. Take your thoughts away from all greed, and then you shall be able to see the wiles (μεθοδείας) of the devil.

166. He who says that he knows all the wiles of the devil speaks as if he did not know himself at all.

167. When the mind (νοῦς) withdraws from bodily cares, in proportion to its withdrawal it sees the craftiness of the enemy.

168. He who is carried away by thoughts is blinded by them. And while he sees the effects of sin, he is unable to see their causes.

169. There is he who is visibly fulfilling commandments, yet is serving a passion, and through evil thoughts is doing away with a good act.

170. Being borne at the beginning of an evil, do not say: "It will not overpower me." For insofar as you are borne by it, to that extent you have been overpowered by it.

171. Everything that happens begins as something small and, being successively sustained, it grows.

172. The way of vice is like an intricate net, and he who is partially entangled in it, if he is negligent, becomes fully tightened up in it.

173. Have no desire to hear about the ill fortune of hostile men. For those who hear such words gather in the fruits of their own disposition.

174. Do not think that every affliction that befalls men is a consequence of sin. For there are some who please God and yet are tempted. Thus, it is written that the ungodly and the iniquitous shall be persecuted (cf. *Psalms* 37:28), and similarly it is written that those who "will live godly in Christ shall suffer persecution" (2 *Timothy* 3:12).

175. At the time of suffering, see the suggestion (προσβολή) of pleasure; for because it relieves the suffering, it becomes acceptable.

176. Some call prudent (φρόνιμοι) those who are

discerning as regards things predictable by the senses. But those are truly prudent who are masters of their own desires.

177. Before the destruction of evils, do not listen to your heart. For it seeks additions similar to what it has within itself.

178. Just as there are serpents which appear in weed-land valleys and others which lurk in houses, so there are passions which assume form in thoughts, and there are others which manifest themselves in action, even if they have changed from one form to another.

179. When you see what is within you moving substantially and inviting the mind to passion while it is still, know that the mind at some time took the lead of them and effected their realization and put them in the heart.

180. A cloud is not formed without the breath of wind; and a passion is not born without a thought.

181. If we no longer "fulfill the desires of the flesh," according to Scripture (*Ephesians* 2:3), what is within us from before will, with the help of the Lord, easily by degrees desist.

182. The substantial images of the mind are more evil and have a firmer hold (or, according to other texts: are stronger). Those connected with thoughts

are their causes and precede them.

183. There is evil which dwells in the heart through the long-continued predisposition, and there is evil which fights us in thought through everyday things.

184. God has regard to our actions according to our intentions. "Grant thee according to thine own heart" (*Psalms* 20:4), says the Lord.

185. He who does not persist in heeding his conscience does not endure bodily suffering for the sake of piety either.

186. Conscience is a natural book. He who reads it actively receives experience of divine help.

187. He who does not voluntarily choose suffering for the sake of truth, will be chastened more painfully by involuntary suffering.

188. He who knows the will of God and does it according to his power, through little suffering will escape greater suffering.

189. He who wishes to overcome temptations without prayer and patient endurance will not drive them away, but will become more entangled with them.

190. The Lord is hidden in His own Command-ments and is found by those who seek Him in pro-portion as they fulfill them.

191. Do not say: "I have fulfilled the Command–ments and have not found the Lord." For you have often found knowledge with righteousness, accord-ing to Scripture. "And those that rightly seek Him shall find peace" (*Proverbs* 16:8 – Septuagint).

192. Peace is deliverance from the passions. It is not found without the action (ἐνέργεια) of the Holy Spirit.

193. Fulfilling a Commandment is one thing, and virtue is another, even though they receive from one another occasions for good.

194. Fulfilling a Commandment means doing what is commanded, whereas virtue is when what is done truly pleases God.

195. Just as visible wealth is one, but is manifold in its acquisition, so virtue is one, but is manifested in many kinds of deeds.

196. He who without deeds makes a display of supposed wisdom and prattles becomes rich through injustice. His labors, according to Scripture, "come into the houses of strangers" (*Proverbs* 5:10 – Septuagint).

197. All things will give way to gold, it is said; and with the grace of God, will be governed by spiritual things.

198. Good conscience is found through prayer; a

pure prayer, through conscience. The one by nature needs the other.

199. Jacob made a coat of many colors for Joseph (*Genesis* 37:3). And the Lord gives knowledge of truth to the meek; as it is written, "the Lord will teach the meek His ways" (*Psalms* 24:9 – Septuagint).

200. Always do the good according to your power. And at the time of the greater good do not turn to the lesser. For Scripture says that "he who turns back is not fit for the Kingdom of Heaven" (*Luke* 9:62).

BY THE SAME SAINT
226 TEXTS
CONCERNING THOSE WHO THINK
THAT MEN ARE JUSTIFIED BY WORKS

1. In the texts which follow, the erroneous faith of those who are outside (true godliness) will be exposed by those who are steadfast in the faith and have discovered the truth.

2. The Lord, wishing to show that every Commandment ought to be fulfilled, and that sonship is granted to men by His own Blood, says: "When ye shall have done those things which are commanded you, say, We are unprofitable servants: we have done that which was our duty to do" (*Luke* 17:10). Wherefore the Kingdom of Heaven is not a reward for works, but a gift of the Master prepared for faithful servants.

3. A servant does not demand freedom as a reward, but gives satisfaction as a debtor and waits for freedom as a gift.

4. "Christ died for our sins," according to the Scriptures (*1 Corinthians* 15:3); and He grants free-

dom to those who serve Him well. For He says: "Well done, thou good and faithful servant; thou hast been faithful over a few things, I will make thee ruler over many things: enter into the joy of the Lord" (*Matthew* 25:21).

5. He who bases himself on bare knowledge is not yet a faithful servant; a faithful servant is he who through obedience believes in Christ, who gave the Commandments.

6. He who honors the Master does what is commanded. When he errs or disobeys, he endures as proper to him whatever befalls him.

7. Being a lover of knowledge, become also a lover of toil. For bare knowledge (ψιλὴ γνῶσις) puffs up man (*1 Corinthians* 8:1).

8. The temptations which occur to us unexpectedly, providentially teach us to become lovers of toil, and draw us to repentance, even when we are not so disposed.

9. The afflictions that befall men are results of their own evils. If we endure them patiently through prayer, we find again the bestowing of good things.

10. Some, having been praised for virtue, were delighted, and they thought that the pleasure of vainglory was divine consolation. Others, having been reproved for sin, were pained, and they viewed the

profitable pain as an action of sin.

11. Those who, on the pretext of struggle, are arrogant towards those who are more negligent, think that they are justified by bodily works. But those of us who, resting on bare knowledge (ψιλὴ γνῶσις) disparage the ignorant, are much more foolish than the first.

12. Without works in accordance with it, knowledge is not yet secure, even if it is true. For of all things the confirmation is by deeds.

13. Often, from negligence with respect to deeds, knowledge becomes darkened. For of those things whose practice has been neglected, the memories in turn will be lost.

14. It is for this reason that Scripture counsels us to know God according to lived knowledge, that we might serve Him rightly through deeds.

15. When we clearly fulfill the Commandments, we both receive from the Lord what is proper in proportion to our fulfilling them, and also are benefited in accordance with the purpose of our choice.

16. He who wants to do something and is unable is, in the sight of God, the knower of hearts, as if he had done it. This is to be understood as regards both good ends and evil ends.

17. The mind (νοῦς) performs many good and evil

acts without the body, whereas the body can do none of these without the mind; because the law of freedom precedes the act.

18. Some, not fulfilling the commandments, think that they believe rightly. Others, fulfilling them, wait for the Kingdom as a reward which is owed to them. Both are mistaken as to the truth.

19. A reward is not something owed to his servants by a master; nor, again, do those who do not serve rightly gain freedom.

20. If "Christ died for us," according to the Scriptures (*Romans* 5:8), and we do not live unto ourselves, but "unto Him which died for us" (*1 Corinthians* 5:15), it is evident that we ought to serve Him unto death. How then are we to reckon sonship as owed to us?

21. Christ is our Master in essence and our Master by dispensation; for when we did not exist, He created us, and when we died through sin He redeemed us through His own Blood, and to those who believe thus He granted His grace.

22. When you hear Scripture saying that "He shall reward every man according to his works" (*Matthew* 16:27), do not think that works are worthy of Gehenna or of the Kingdom, but that Christ rewards each one according to his works of faith or lack of faith in

Him, not as being an exchanger of things, but as being God our Creator and Redeemer.

23. Those of us who have been deemed worthy of the washing of regeneration offer good works not for recompense, but for the preservation of the purity that has been given us.

24. Every good work which we perform through our own nature makes us refrain from the opposite, but without grace is incapable of adding to our sanctification.

25. The self-restrained man abstains from gluttony; he who has renounced property abstains from greed; he who is still abstains from talkativeness; he who is pure abstains from love of pleasure; he who is chaste abstains from fornication; he who is self-sufficient abstains from love of money; he who is meek abstains from agitation; he who is humble abstains from vainglory; he who is obedient abstains from contentiousness; he who is reprieving abstains from hypocrisy. Similarly, he who prays abstains from hopelessness; the poor, from greatness of wealth; the person who confesses; from denial; the martyr, from idolatry. Do you see how every virtue that is performed, even unto death, is nothing else than abstinence from sin? Now abstinence from sin is a work of nature, not an exchange for the Kingdom.

26. Man scarcely preserves what is proper to his nature; but Christ grants sonship through the Cross.

27. There is a Commandment which is special, and there is another which is comprehensive. By the former He enjoins specially to "impart to him that hath none" (*Luke* 3:11); by the latter, He commands renouncing all that one has (*Luke* 14:33).

28. There is an action of grace, not known to the "child," and there is another action, that of vice, which resembles truth. It is good not to look at these as in a mirror, because of the possibility of deception, and not to curse them, because of the possibility of truth, but with hope to bring all to God, for He knows the helpfulness of both.

29. He who wants to cross the spiritual sea, exercises long-suffering, humility, vigilance, and self-restraint. If he presses to enter it without these four virtues he disturbs his heart, but is unable to cross.

30. Quietude (ἡσυχία) is a cessation of evils. If one also adds to prayer the four virtues, there is no help that is a shorter way to freedom from passions.

31. It is not possible for the mind to be quiet (ἡσυχάσαι) without the body being quiet also. Nor is it possible to destroy their dividing wall without quietude and prayer.

32. 'The flesh desireth against the Spirit, and the

Spirit against the flesh' (*Galatians* 5:17). Those who "walk in the Spirit shall not fulfill the desire of the flesh" (*Galatians* 5:16).

33. There is no perfect prayer without mental invocation (ἐπίκλησις). And when thought cries aloud without distraction, the Lord will listen.

34. When the mind prays without distraction, it afflicts the heart. And "a broken and humbled heart God will not despise" (*Psalms* 50:17—Septuagint).

35. Prayer, too, is called a virtue, even though it is the mother of the virtues. For it produces them through union with Christ.

36. Whatever we do without prayer and good hope, afterward turns out to be hurtful and imperfect.

37. When you hear that the "first shall be last, and the last shall be first" (*Matthew* 19:30), understand this to refer to partakers of the virtues and partakers of love. For love is the last of the virtues in the order of acquisition, but is the first in the order of value, showing those which preceded it to be last in that order.

38. If you become despondent during prayer, or in various ways afflicted by badness, remember the departure at death and the sufferings of hell. But it is better "to cleave close to God" through prayer and hope (*Psalms* 72:28—Septuagint), than to have secular

remembrances, even though these might be helpful.

39. None of the virtues alone, by itself, opens our natural door (to salvation). Being interdependent, the virtues act as a unity.

40. He who is nourished by thoughts is not self-restrained. For even if they should be profitable, they are not more profitable than hope.

41. Every sin for which one does not repent is unto death. About this, even if a Saint should pray for another, he will not be heard.

42. He who repents rightly does not reckon the toil against his former sins, but through it propitiates God.

43. If it were our duty to perform daily all the good acts which are proper to our nature, then what shall we offer to God in repayment for our evil acts that were done before?

44. Whatever the preeminence of our virtuous acts of today might be, when our negligence is gone, it is a reproof, not a recompense.

45. He who is afflicted mentally and rests physically is like him who is afflicted physically and is relaxed mentally.

46. Voluntary suffering of either the body or the mind contributes to that of the other: that of the mind to that of the flesh, and that of the flesh to that of

the mind. the combination of the two becomes more painful.

47. It is a great virtue to endure patiently whatever befalls you and to love your neighbor who hates you, according to the word of the Lord (*Matthew* 5:44).

48. A sign of love without dissimulation is forgiveness of offences. For it is in such a way that the Lord also loved the world.

49. It is not possible to forgive someone's offences with one's heart without true knowledge. For the latter shows to each one that what befalls him is his own.

50. You will lose none of the things which you give up for the Lord. For at the proper time it will come to you manifold.

51. When the mind forgets the aim (τὸν σκοπόν) of piety, then visible work of virtue becomes unprofitable.

52. If evil counsel is harmful to every man, it is much more so to those who have entered upon the path of strictness (ἀκρίβεια).

53. Philosophize in deed concerning the will of man and the retribution of God. For words are not wiser or more profitable than deeds.

54. Effort for the sake of piety is followed by help from God. One must know this through divine law and conscience.

55. A certain man received a thought, and without examining it retained it. Another man received a thought and truly examined it. One must reflect which of the two men acted in a more pious manner.

56. True knowledge is to endure patiently afflictions and not to blame men for one's own misfortunes.

57. He who does a good deed and asks for recompense is not serving God but his own will.

58. It is not possible for him who has sinned to escape retribution, except through repentance appropriate to his error.

59. Some say: "We are unable to do good unless we actively receive the Grace of the Spirit.

60. Always those who by choice are involved in pleasures refuse to do what is in their power because they are not aided (by Grace).

61. Grace is granted mystically to those who have been baptized into Christ; but it acts in proportion to the fulfilling of the Commandments. Grace never ceases helping us secretly; but it is up to us to do good according to our power.

62. Firstly, it arouses conscience in a manner becoming God. Wherefore even evil-doers, upon repenting, pleased God.

63. Again, Grace is hidden in the act of teaching

our neighbor. There are times when reading, it accompanies the intellect. And by natural consequence it teaches its own truth. If we do not hide talent of this consequence, we shall actually enter in to the joy of the Lord.

64. He who seeks the energies of God before doing what the Commandments enjoin is like a slave who as soon as he has been redeemed from slavery wants to receive a letter stating his freedom.

65. He who has found external attacks occurring through Divine justice, in seeking the Lord found knowledge together with justice.

66. If you comprehend, according to Scripture, that on the whole earth there are the Judgments of God, then every misfortune will serve to us as a teacher.

67. How each thing is to be treated is specified by its nature. But only God knows the variety of appropriate visitations.

68. When you are subjected to a dishonor by men, immediately perceive some honor from God. The dishonor will not cause you to experience sorrow and perturbations. And as far as the honor from God is concerned, you will remain faithful and irreproachable when it comes.

69. When you are praised by a multitude by God's good will, do not exhibit any ostentation, whereby

you will fall from honor to dishonor.

70. A seed will not sprout without earth and water; and a man will not benefit without voluntary hardships.

71. It is not possible to have rain without clouds, or to please God without a good conscience.

72. Do not refuse to learn, even if you happen to be prudent. For God's dispensation is more beneficent than our prudence.

73. When the heart, prompted by a certain pleasure, abandons love of painful efforts, then one will slip downward as if drawn by a very heavy stone that rolls downward.

74. An inexperienced calf, running towards herbs, ends up at a precipitous place. Such is a soul that finds itself gradually led astray by thoughts.

75. When the mind has grown strong in the Lord, it detaches itself from chronic sinful preconceptions. Then the heart is as if tortured by executioners who draw it hither and thither, that is, the mind and the passion.

76. Just as those who are sailing at sea gladly endure the burning heat of the sun, sustained by their hope or profit, so those who hate vice love criticism of themselves. The first oppose the strong winds, while the second opposes the passions.

77. Just as flight in winter or on the Sabbath is painful to the flesh and profanation to the soul, likewise is an uprising of the passions in an aged body to a consecrated soul.

78. No one is as good and compassionate as the Lord. But even He does not forgive a person who does not repent.

79. Many of us are sorry for our sins, but gladly assent to their causes.

80. A mole, crawling under the ground, being blind cannot see the stars; and he who does not have faith for transitory things cannot have faith for the eternal either.

81. True knowledge (γνῶσῃ) is given to man as a gift prior to Grace. This knowledge teaches above all those who accept it to believe in its bestower, God.

82. Whenever a sinful soul does not accept the afflictions which befall it, then the Angels say about it: "We cured Babylon and she was not cured." (*Jeremiah* 28:9).

83. A mind which forgets true knowledge fights in favor of things which are contrary to its true interest, as if they were in the interest of human beings.

84. Just as fire cannot endure in water, so shameful thoughts cannot abide in a God-loving heart. For every God-loving individual is also a lover of volun-

tary effort, and voluntary effort is by nature opposed to pleasure.

85. A passion which has prevailed by choice, on a second occasion violently prevails, even if he who has it does not want it to have its way.

86. We like the causes of involuntary thoughts. For this reason they occur; whereas the occurrence of voluntary thoughts is prompted also by things themselves.

87. Conceit and arrogance are causes of blasphemy. Avarice and vanity are causes of pitilessness and hypocrisy.

88. When the devil sees that the mind has prayed with the heart, he gives rise to great and cunning temptations. For he is not oriented to destroying small virtues by means of great assaults.

89. A thought which lingers in the mind indicates an individual's passionate inclination towards it, whereas a banishment of it signifies opposition to it and war against it.

90. There are three mental places (νοητοὶ τόποι) where the mind enters through change: that which is according to nature, that which is above nature, and that which is contrary to nature. When it enters that which is according to nature, it finds itself the cause of evil thoughts, and confesses to God its sins, know-

ing the causes of the passions. When it enters the place that is "contrary to nature" it forgets the justice of God, and quarrels with men, that supposedly are unjust to him. When he comes to the place that is "above nature" it finds the fruits of the Holy Spirit, which the Apostle calls love, joy, peace, and so forth. And he knows that if he prefers bodily cares, he cannot abide there. And he who departs from that place, that is, from the place "above nature," falls into sin and the accompanying dreadful events, and if not soon, at the time when known to God's justice.

91. The knowledge of each individual is true in proportion as it is confirmed by meekness, humility, and love.

92. Everyone who has been Baptized in the Orthodox way has mystically received all Grace. He is informed about this while fulfilling the Commandments.

93. A Commandment of Christ fulfilled in accordance with conscience and wholeheartedly is rewarded. But the reward comes at the appropriate time.

94. Have steadfast prayer in everything you undertake to do, so that you will never do anything without the help of God.

95. Nothing is stronger in efficacy than prayer; and for God's favor there is nothing that is better.

96. Every act that is in accord with the Command–ments is contained in praying, for there is nothing higher than love of God.

97. Prayer without a wandering of the mind is a sign of love of God. On the other hand, neglect of prayer and wandering of the mind is a token of love of pleasure.

98. He who takes part in vigils and prays without experiencing discomfort is clearly a partaker of the Grace of the Holy Spirit. He, on the other hand, who is afflicted by pain and voluntarily abides in them will quickly receive Divine help.

99. One Commandment differs from another Commandment. And faith differs from faith, and one faith is more secure and unshakable than another.

100. There is faith that originates from hearing and there is faith which is the substance of things hoped for. (*Romans* 10:17, *Hebrews* 11:1).

101. It is good to persuade through words those who enquire. Better than this is to edify through prayer and virtue. For through these one commends himself to God, and he helps his neighbor.

102. If you want with words to benefit one who loves to learn, suggest to him prayer, true faith, and patience with regard to the things that happen. For all good events take place through these three.

103. With regard to those things for which he has hope in God, one does not argue with others.

104. If everything involuntary has as its cause acts that are voluntary, then no one is such an enemy of a man as is a man himself.

105. Of all evils the first is ignorance; next after this is unbelief.

106. Flee from temptation through patience and prayer. If you remain without these, the temptation comes with greater intensity.

107. He who is meek according to God is wiser than the wise; and he who is humble in heart is stronger than the strong. For they bear according to knowledge the yoke of Christ.

108. All the things that we do without prayer, later turn out to be either faulty or harmful, and by events criticize us.

109. One becomes righteous through deeds, words, and thoughts. And through faith, grace, and repentance many become righteous.

110. Just as pride is something alien to one who is repenting, so it is impossible for one who is voluntarily sinning to be humble-minded.

111. Humility is not condemnation by one's conscience; it is God's grace and a consciousness of His sympathy.

112. What the house is for the air, so is the mind for Divine grace. And the more you remove material things from the house, the more does air come in; and the more you bring things into the house the more does the air leave the house.

113. Matter of the house consists in the furniture and the foods. The matter of the mind comprises vainglory and pleasure.

114. Hope in God constitutes ample room in the heart. Bodily cares constitute narrow space.

115. The grace of the Spirit is one and unalterable; It acts in the case of each individual as it wishes.

116. Just as heavy rain falling on the earth is conducive to a good condition of the plants, promoting the special qualities of each one, likewise grace does good to the hearts of the faithful: it imparts to the virtues appropriate energies.

117. When grace comes to the heart of one who hungers for Christ, it becomes food; to one who thirsts for Christ, it becomes an exceedingly sweet drink; to him who is cold, clothing; to him who is laboring, rest; to him who is praying, intimation; and to him who is mourning, consolation.

118. When you hear Scripture saying about the Holy Spirit that It sat on each one of the Apostles (*Acts of the Apostles* 2), or that It "rushed on the

Prophet" (*1 Kings* 11:6, 16:13), or that It acts, or that It is sorry, or that It is quenched, or that It is irritated; and again, when you hear it saying that "some have the first fruits," while "are full of the Holy Spirit," still, believe in the manner which we spoke of earlier, namely that the Holy Spirit is unchanging and omnipotent. In Its energies It is that which It is, and to each one It provides that which is proper for God to provide. For the Spirit has shone fully like the sun upon those baptized. Each one is illuminated in proportion as he has hated the passions which darken his soul, and has gotten rid of them. And in proportion as one loves them it is darkened.

119. He who hates the passions removes their causes. He, on the other hand, who is surrounded by their causes is fought against by the passions, even when he does not want them.

120. When we are attacked by evil thoughts, we should blame ourselves and not ancestral sin.

121. Roots of evil thoughts are obvious vices which we defend on each occasion with our hands, with our feet, and with our mouth.

122. It is not possible for us to occupy ourselves mentally with familiarity with some passion is we do not like its causes.

123. Who is there that endures disgrace and occu-

pies himself mentally with vainglory? And who is there that likes humiliation and is upset when they insult him? And who is there whose heart is full of compunction and humility and assents to carnal pleasure? Or, who believes in Christ and concerns himself with transitory things?

124. He who is disapproved of by another and does not quarrel with him by means of words, or thoughts, possesses true spiritual knowledge, and shows firm faith in the Lord.

125. Men cheat in weighing, doing injustice, but God gives to each one that which is just.

126. If neither He who does injustice has superfluity, nor he who suffers injustice is in want, then man goes through life as an image of a dream, and hence in vain is he perturbed (*Psalms* 38:7).

127. When you see someone who is worrying because he has been greatly insulted, know that having been filled with vainglorious thoughts, now with disgust and aversion he reaps what he sowed in his heart.

128. He who has enjoyed bodily pleasures beyond measure will pay a hundredfold with sorrows and distress for the excess.

129. The spiritual guide should tell him who is under his care his duties; and when he disobeys his

spiritual guide, the latter should foretell him the coming raid of evils.

130. He who suffers injustice from someone and does not seek a rectification of the injustice shows that he believes in Christ, and he receives a hundred-fold recompense in the present life and inherits life eternal.

131. Remembrance of God is an exertion of the heart for the sake of piety. Everyone who forgets God focuses on pleasures and becomes unfeeling.

132. Do not say that whoever is passionless cannot feel sorrow; for if he does not feel sorrow for himself, he ought to feel sorrow for his neighbor.

133. When the enemy holds in his hands many accounts of sins that had been forgotten, he forces the debtor to do the same sins in memory, using the law of sin.

134. If you want to remember God unceasingly, do not repel as unjust the sorrows that come to you as unjust, but endure them, reflecting that they come justly. For patience with every sorrow awakens memory, whereas mental indolence lessens the mindset of the heart and leads to forgetting God.

135. If you want your sins to be covered by the Lord (cf. *Psalms* 32:1), do not reveal to men that you have virtue. For whatever we do with regard to the

latter, God will also do with regard to the former.

136. Having hidden your virtue, do not exalt yourself as fulfilling righteousness. For righteousness is not only to hide one's good deeds, but also to think of none of the things that are forbidden.

137. Do not rejoice when you do something good for someone, but when you endure without malice the accompanying adversity. For hurt follows benefaction in the same way that night follows day.

138. Vainglory, love of money, and pleasure do not leave benefaction spotless, unless they have previously fallen through fear of God.

139. The mercy of God is hidden in involuntary pains, drawing to repentance him who endures them patiently and delivering him from everlasting hell.

140. Some, fulfilling the Commandments, expect this to counterpoise their sins in a balance; others propitiate through them Him who died for our sins. One must enquire which of these men has the right view.

141. The fear of Gehenna and the eros of the Kingdom give the power to endure afflictions. And this, not through themselves, but through Him who knows our thoughts (cf. *Matthew* 5:22).

142. He who has faith concerning future things abstains of his own accord from pleasures. But he

who lacks faith becomes a pleasure seeker and hard-hearted.

143. Do not say: "How will a poor man lead a plea-sure-loving life, not having the presuppositions?" For one can also lead a pleasure-loving life more pitifully through thoughts.

144. Knowledge of things is one thing, and knowl-edge of truth is another. The second is more prof-itable than the first to the same extent that the sun surpasses the moon.

145. Knowledge of things comes to one in propor-tion as he fulfills the Commandments; but knowl-edge of truth comes in proportion to one's hope in Christ.

146. If you wish to be saved and "to come unto knowledge of the truth" (*1 Timothy* 2:4), endeavor always to transcend things apprended by the sens-es, and through hope alone to cleave to God. If you deviate from this way, you will find demonic prin-cipalities and powers fighting against you through suggestions. Prevailing over them through prayer and hope, you shall have God's grace delivering you from the wrath to come.

147. He who understands that which has been said in a mystical sense by St. Paul, that the wrestling is against "spiritual wickedness" (*Ephesians* 6:12), will

also understand the parable of the Lord, which He spoke to this end, that men ought always to pray, and not to faint (*Luke* 18:1).

148. The Law prescribes formally (to men) six days to labor and on the seventh day to have rest (*Exodus* 20:9). For the "labor" of the soul is beneficence by means of money, that is, by means of things. Its "rest" and calm is to sell everything and "give to the poor" (*Matthew* 19:21) and, having through the non-possession of property stopped labor, to have rest in spiritual hope. Therefore Paul also exhorts us to enter with haste into that rest, saying: "Let us labor to enter into that rest" (*Hebrews* 4:11).

149. We have said this without excluding the things to come, nor limiting general retribution to the present life, but only asserting that it is necessary in the first place to have the grace of the Holy Spirit acting in the heart, and thus to enter in proportion (to our participation in it) into the Kingdom of Heaven. Revealing this, the Lord said: "The Kingdom of Heaven is within you" (*Luke* 17:21). And the Apostle, too, said this: "Faith is the substance of things hoped for" (*Hebrews* 11:1); again: "Run, that ye may obtain" (*1 Corinthians* 9:24); and again: "Prove yourselves, whether ye be in the faith. Know ye not how that Jesus Christ is in you, except ye be reprobate?" (2

Corinthians 13:5).

150. He who has come to know the truth does not set himself against afflicting happenings. For he knows that these lead man to fear of God.

151. Former sins when remembered in detail (or: individually) do harm to the hopeful man. For when they issue forth with sorrow they weaken hope, while when they are represented without sorrow they deposit the old defilement.

152. When the mind through self-denial keeps unwavering hope, then the enemy, on the pretext of confession, pictures one's former sins, in order that he might rekindle the passions which through the grace of God have been forgotten. For then, if both strong and passion-hating, the mind will of necessity be darkened, having become confused over the things that have taken place. And if the mind should still be foggy and pleasure-loving, it will at all events tarry and passionately have converse with the suggestions. Thus, such a memory will be found to be a predisposition and not a confession.

153. If you wish to offer to God confession free from condemnation, do not recall your deviations in detail, but stand firmly and nobly against their allurement.

154. Troublesome things come as a result of former

sins, bringing what is akin to each trespass.

155. He who is wise and knows the truth confesses to God not through the remembrance of the things that were done, but by enduring what befalls him.

156. If you cast away suffering and dishonor, do not profess that you are confessing through other virtues. For vainglory and hard-heartedness are by nature disposed to serve sin, even by means of things of the light.

157. Just as suffering and dishonor are wont to bring forth the virtues, so pleasure and vainglory are wont to bring forth the vices.

158. Every bodily pleasure results from prior ease. And ease is born of lack of faith.

159. He who is under the power of sin cannot alone prevail over carnal thought, because he has the provocation unceasingly and in his members.

160. Those who are passionate must pray and be obedient. For it is barely possible (for them) with help to fight against their predispositions (προλήψεις).

161. He who strikes desire with obedience and prayer is a methodical athlete, clearly exhibiting mental wrestling through abstinence from sensory things.

162. He who does not reconcile his will with God is tripped up in his own pursuits and comes under

the control of his adversaries.

163. When you see two wicked men having love for one another, know that each of them contributes to the bad desires of the other.

164. The proud man and the vainglorious man associate with one another with pleasure; for the proud man praises the vainglorious man when the latter servilely cringes before him; while the vainglorious magnifies the proud man who continually praises him.

165. The God-loving hearer derives benefit from both instances: when he is reminded of his good deeds, he becomes more zealous, and when he is reproved for sins, he is forced to repent. We ought to lead a life in accordance with our progress, and in accordance with our life we ought to offer our prayers to God.

166. It is good to hold fast the principal Commandment and not to take thought for, nor pray for anything else, but only to seek the Kingdom and the word of God (*Matthew* 6:33). If we still take thought for every necessity, we ought also to pray for every necessity. He who does take thought for something without prayer is not successful with regard to the purpose of his endeavor. And this is the meaning of the Lord's statement: "Without me ye can do noth-

ing" (*John* 15:5).

167. In the case of the man who leaves out of reckoning the Commandment regarding prayer, harmful acts of disobedience follow, one leading him like a captive to another.

168. He who accepts present afflictions with the expectation of future goods has attained to knowledge of truth; and he will be freed easily from anger and grief.

169. He who chooses maltreatment and dishonor for the sake of truth is walking on the Apostolic path, having taken up the cross and being bound with a chain (cf. *Matthew* 16:24; *Acts of the Apostles* 28:20). He who attempts to turn his attention to the heart without these goes astray mentally and falls into the temptations and snares of the devil (cf. *1 Timothy* 3:7; 6:9).

170. He who fights can never overcome evil thoughts without overcoming their causes, nor their causes without the thoughts. For when we cast away one of them in a one-sided manner, not long afterwards we will be full of both through the other.

171. He who fights against men through fear of suffering and reproach, either suffers here more through events or is mercilessly punished in the age to come.

172. He who wishes to exclude every bad event ought through prayer to reconcile himself with God, and on the one hand retain mentally hope in Him, and on the other hand, as far as possible, diminish concern about things perceptible by the senses.

173. When the devil finds a man who is preoccupied unnecessarily with bodily things, first he snatches away the spoils of knowledge; then he cuts off, as a head, hope in God.

174. If you should ever receive a secure place (in other texts: a method) of pure prayer, do not accept at that time the knowledge of things which is given by the enemy, lest you lose what is greater. For it is better to strike him down with the arrows of prayer, while he is shut up somewhere below, than to hold converse with him as he is offering evil things and scheming to tear you away from prayer against him.

175. Knowledge of things is of benefit to man during temptation and despondency; but during prayer it is wont to be very harmful.

176. Having had the lot to teach in the Lord and be disobeyed, grieve mentally but be not disturbed visibly. For being afflicted, you will not be condemned together with the one who is disobeying; but if you are disturbed you will be tempted in the same

thing.

177. At the time of explanation do not hide what is proper to those present: giving a clearer account of the things which are seemly, and a vaguer one of the things which are harsh.

178. Do not bring before one who is not subordinate to you his fault. For this is a matter of authority rather than of counsel.

179. What is said in the plural becomes profitable to all, showing to each one what is proper to him according to conscience.

180. He who speaks rightly ought himself also to speak as receiving what he says from God. For truth is not the speaker's but is God's, Who is acting (in him).

181. Do not dispute with those from whom you do not have a confession of obedience when they are set against the truth, lest you arouse hatred, according to Scripture (cf. *Proverbs* 9:8).

182. He who gives way, where he should not, to one who is under obedience to him, when that person contradicts him, leads that person astray as regards that thing and prepares him to set at naught the covenant of obedience.

183. He who with fear of God admonishes or instructs a man who sins preserves for himself the vir-

tue that is opposed to the fault. On the other hand, the person who bears malice and malevolently reproaches him, falls into the same passion, according to spiritual law.

184. He who has learned the law well fears the lawgiver, and fearing him turns away from every evil (cf. *Proverbs* 15:27).

185. Do not become double-tongued, being disposed in one way in word and in another way in conscience. For Scripture places such a one under curse (cf. *Wisdom of Sirach* 28:13).

186. There is a man who speaks the truth and is hated by the foolish, according to the Apostle (cf. *Proverbs* 10:1; this statement is not found in the Apostolic texts). And there is a man who pretends, and for this reason is loved. What is due to each does not take long to come, for the Lord renders to each at the appropriate time what is due.

187. He who wishes to avoid future hardships ought to endure gladly present ones. For in this way, exchanging mentally one thing for another, through small pains one will avoid great punishments.

188. Secure your speech from boasting and your thoughts from conceit, lest you be abandoned and do adverse things. For the good is not accomplished fully by man alone, but by the all-seeing God.

189. The all-seeing God renders due happenings for our deeds, and similarly for our thoughts and our voluntary conceptions.

190. Involuntary thoughts arise from preceding sin; voluntary ones, from our free will. Hence, the latter are seen to be the causes of the former.

191. Grief accompanies thoughts which are unintentionally evil; wherefore they soon disappear. But joy accompanies those which are so intentionally; wherefore they become difficult to get rid of.

192. The pleasure-loving man is grieved by censure and sufferings; whereas the God-loving man is grieved by praises and advantages.

193. He who does not know the judgments of God mentally walks on a road with cliffs all around and is easily upset by every wind. When he is praised, he bears himself proudly; when he is censured, he is embittered. When he feasts, he behaves licentiously; and when he suffers, he laments bitterly. When he understands, he likes to show off; and when he does not understand, he pretends (to understand). When he is rich, he is boastful; and when he is poor, he feigns. When he is satiated, he is bold; and when he fasts, he is vainglorious. He quarrels with those who reprove him, and regards as foolish those who grant him forgiveness.

194. If then one does not acquire, through the grace of Christ, knowledge of truth and fear of God, he is wounded terribly not only by the passions, but also by untoward happenings.

195. When you want to loose an entangled thing, seek about it what pleases God, and you will find the unloosing of it profitable.

196. In whatever things God takes pleasure, these also the whole of creation serves. And from whatever things He turns away, these the creation also opposes.

197. He who resists sad happenings unwittingly opposes the command of God. But he who accepts them with true knowledge, he, according to Scripture "waits on the Lord" (*Psalm* 27:14).

198. When temptation comes, do not seek (to find out) why or through whom it came, but only to endure it gratefully, without sorrow and without bearing malice.

199. Another's sin does not add to ours, unless we accept it with evil thoughts.

200. If it is not possible easily to find a man who has pleased (God) without temptations, we ought to thank God for everything that happens to us.

201. If Peter had not failed in the night's fishing (*Luke* 5:5), he would not have succeeded in that of

daytime. And if Paul had not suffered physical blindness (*Acts of the Apostles* 9:8), he would not have opened up his spiritual eyes. And if Stephen had not been slandered (*Ibid* 6:13) as a blasphemer, he would not have seen God, the heavens being opened.

202. Just as work according to God is called virtue, so unexpected affliction is called temptation.

203. God tempted Abraham (*Genesis* 22:1 ff.), that is, He afflicted him for his benefit, not in order that He may learn the character of Abraham—for He knew him, for He knows all things before their coming into being—but in order that He may provide him with occasions for perfect faith.

204. Every affliction exposes the propensity of the will, whether it inclines to the right or to the left. This is why chance affliction is called temptation, because it provides to the partaker experience of his hidden desires.

205. The fear of God compels us to fight against vice; and when we fight, the grace of God fights against it (in other texts: destroys it).

206. Wisdom is not only to know the truth through natural sequence, but also to endure as one's own the wickedness of those who wrong us. For those who remained in (i.e. did not go beyond) the former were roused to pride, whereas those who attained to the

latter acquired humility.

207. If you wish not to be acted upon by evil thoughts, accept contempt of soul and suffering of the flesh. And this not on particular occasions, but at every time and place and in all things.

208. He who is brought up in voluntary suffering will not be dominated by involuntary thoughts; whereas he who does not accept the former is taken prisoner by the latter, even when he does not wish.

209. When, upon being wronged, your feelings and heart are hardened, do not grieve, because this has happened providentially; instead, rejoicing, overturn the thoughts that rise up, knowing that if these are destroyed at the stage when they are suggestions, after the movement the evil also will by nature be destroyed together with them; whereas if the thoughts continue, the evil, too, is wont to grow.

210. Without contrition of the heart it is, in general, impossible to be freed from vice. Now the heart is made contrite by threefold self-restraint: I mean that with respect to sleep, to food, and to bodily rest. For excess of these instills voluptuousness, and voluptuousness accepts evil thoughts; also it is opposed to prayer and to proper service.

211. It having fallen to your lot to give orders to your brethren, keep your position and do not pass

over in silence what is needful because of those who contradict you. In those matters in which they obey, you will have a reward for their virtue; while in those matters in which they disobey, you will at all events forgive them, and you will receive an equal reward from Him who has said: forgive and it shall be forgiven you (cf. *Matthew* 6:14).

212. Every happening is like a trading-fair. He who knows how to engage in business derives much profit, whereas he who does not, suffers losses.

213. Do not compel with contentiousness him who has not obeyed one of your precepts, but lay up for yourself the gain which he threw away. Forbearance will benefit you more than his correction.

214. When the harm of one affects many, then you must not be long-suffering, nor seek your own interest, but that of the many, in order that they might be saved. For virtue which has reference to many is more useful than virtue which has reference to one.

215. If one falls into any sin whatsoever and does not grieve in proportion to the fall, he will easily fall again into the same net.

216. Just as a lioness does not amicably let a heifer come near her, so shamelessness does not with good will accept grief according to God.

217. Just as a sheep does not come together with

a wolf for procreation, so pain of the heart does not couple with satiety for the conception of virtue.

218. No one can have suffering and grief according to God, unless he has previously loved the causes of these.

219. Fear of God and self-examination may occasion grief. And self-restraint and vigilance are conversant with suffering.

220. He who is not instructed in the Scriptural commandments and admonitions will be plagued as by the horse's whip and the donkey's goad (cf. *Proverbs* 26:3).

221. He who is easily overcome by small things is necessarily enslaved by big ones also. But he who despises small things will oppose great ones aided by the Lord.

222. Do not attempt to benefit through reproofs one who is boasting of his virtues. For the same man cannot be both fond of showing off and a lover of truth.

223. Every word of Christ displays God's mercy, justice and wisdom, and through hearing introduces the power of these into those who hear them gladly. Wherefore the unmerciful and the unjust, hearing without pleasure, were not able to know the wisdom of God, but even crucified Him for teaching

it. Let us also observe whether we hear Him gladly (cf. *Mark* 12:37). For He says: "He that loves me will keep my commandments, and he shall be loved of my Father, and I will love him, and will manifest myself to him" (*John* 14:21). Do you see how He hid His manifestation in the Commandments? Of all the Commandments, therefore, that of love for God and for neighbor is the most comprehensive. This love is made firm by abstinence from worldly things and by stillness of the thoughts.

224. Knowing this, the Lord enjoins us saying: "Take no thought for the morrow" (*Matthew* 6:34); and reasonably. For how will he who has not freed himself from worldly things and anxiety about them, be freed from evil thoughts? And how will he who is surrounded by such thoughts see the inherent sin concealed in him? This sin is the darkness and fog of the soul. It has had its beginning in evil thoughts and deeds, was on the one hand the devil, tempting through suggestion, and intimating the beginning. On the other hand, man with pleasure holding converse with the suggestion through love of pleasure and vainglory—for even if according to his discernment he did not wish it, nevertheless in actuality he felt pleasure and accepted it. If one has not seen this comprehensive sin, when will he pray regarding it

and be cleansed? And how will he who has not been cleansed find the place of pure nature? And how will he who has not found this behold the inner house of Christ? For we are a house of God, according to the Prophetic, Evangelical and Apostolic saying (*Hebrews* 3:6).

225. It follows then from what has already been said that it is necessary to seek and find the house; and standing fast through prayer, to knock, in order that either now or at our departure the Master might open to us and not say, because of our neglect: "I know not whence ye are" (*Luke* 13:25). Not only ought we to seek and receive, but having received, we ought to preserve what is given. For there are some who after receiving, lost what was given. Wherefore, perhaps both persons late in learning and also young persons possess bare knowledge or chance experience of the aforementioned things. But only the devout and much experienced among the old possess steadfast work together with patient endurance, having often lost it through carelessness. And voluntarily suffered, searched for it, and found it. Let us, too, therefore, not cease doing the latter, until we make it a possession of ours not to be taken away.

226. We have come to know these few ordinances—out of the many—of the Spiritual Law. These the

great Psalmist (*Psalms* 1:2; 118:16, 23, 71, 112) also ever teaches those who chant them in the Lord Jesus, to learn and fulfill. To Him is due glory and power and worship, both now and unto the ages. Amen.

INDEX